ISLAM

-

Three Core Beliefs

-

Tawheed : Oneness of Allah

Risalah : Prophethood

Aakhirah : Life Hereafter

Syed Abul Hasan 'Ali Nadwi

Translated by
Mohammed Moidul Haque

Table of Contents

Translator's Note

All praise be to Allah, the Cherisher and Sustainer of the worlds, and His blessings be on Prophet Muhammad, his progeny and his Companions

This is the English translation of the book *Islam ke Teen Bunyadi 'Aqaaid*[1] which was originally written in Urdu by Syed Abul Hasan 'Ali Nadwi. It focuses on three core elements of *'aqeedah* (faith) of Islam: *Tawheed* (oneness of Allah), *risalah* (prophethood) and *aakhirah* (Life Hereafter). These three elements of faith serve as the very foundation upon which the entire structure of Islam stands.

Allah is the sole creator, controller and sustainer of the universe and whatever it contains. He has no partner and no one shares any power with Him. He is not dependent on anyone, but everyone else is dependent on Him. This is the essence of *Tawheed*.

This life is very short and every soul which has come into existence will die one day. Then there will be the Day of Judgment when everyone will be resurrected, accounted for every action that he did in this life, rewarded or punished accordingly and entered into the Life Hereafter which will last forever.

To make humans aware of Himself, the Life Hereafter and consequences of their deeds, Allah sent prophets, Adam being the first and Muhammad being the last of them. Without the guidance of prophets, it is not possible for humans to know who Allah is and what the Life Hereafter entails.

Thus a clear understanding of the attributes of Allah, the Life Hereafter and the role and status of prophets is very essential to fully and correctly understand Islam. This book explains these topics in a very methodical way with the help of Quranic verses and authentic *ahadith* (sayings and practices of Prophet Muhammad).

Since Arabic terms (such as *'aqeedah, deen, iman, risalah,* etc.) are becoming more common in English Islamic literature and it is very difficult to find exact equivalent English words for them, I have used them frequently in this translation. However, to aid the readers in understanding

---

[1] اسلام کےتین بنيادي عقائد

these terms, I have given (only for the first instance in most cases) their meaning in English in parentheses and displayed them in Arabic script in the footnote; the glossary at the end of the book lists all such terms in Arabic script with their meaning in English. For the English equivalent of an Arabic term, I have relied mainly on Hans Wehr's *A Dictionary of Modern Written Arabic* (3rd Edition).

I am grateful to Syed Bilal 'Abdul Hai Hasani Nadwi (publisher of the Urdu version) who was kind enough to grant me permission to translate and publish this book. I must also thank everyone who has helped me by providing valuable support in editing and proof reading. May Allah accept this effort and reward everyone who has participated in any form in completing this work! May Allah make it a means for the readers to correctly understand *Tawheed, risalah, aakhirah* and the status of Prophet Muhammad as the final prophet!

Please send your comments and suggestions to mmhaque15@gmail.com.

Mohammed Moidul Haque, Ph.D.   25th August 2014 AD
Former Professor of Computer Science
Northeastern Illinois University
Chicago, USA

Preface

The very first and foremost demand that Islam makes of its adherents is to correct and purify their 'aqeedah[1] (faith). In fact, 'aqeedah was the main focus of the mission of every prophet from Prophet Adam (the first prophet) to Prophet Muhammad (the last prophet). They invited people towards 'aqeedah with full conviction and devotion. They never tolerated any alteration or deviation in it. They never subscribed to any personality, philosophy, way of life, or system of governance, regardless of how revolutionary or charismatic it was, if it did not conform to correct 'aqeedah. It is in fact the 'aqeedah that sets prophets apart from the political and social leaders of their time.

The Holy Quran and *seerah*[2] (life) of Prophet Muhammad (saw[3]) are full of examples of how prophets struggled and sacrificed to inculcate correct 'aqeedah in people.

In the following verse of the Holy Quran, Allah has praised Prophet Ibrahim[4] (*alaihis salaam*[5]) for the concern and compassion that he had for his people:

$$إِنَّ إِبْرَاهِيمَ لَحَلِيمٌ أَوَّاهٌ مُّنِيبٌ$$

Indeed, Ibrahim was kind, compassionate, and penitent. [Hud, 11:75]

A similar description of Prophet Ibrahim's companions is found in the following verse:

$$قَدْ كَانَتْ لَكُمْ أُسْوَةٌ حَسَنَةٌ فِى إِبْرَاهِيمَ وَٱلَّذِينَ مَعَهُ إِذْ قَالُوا$$
$$لِقَوْمِهِمْ إِنَّا بُرَءَاؤُا۟ مِنكُمْ وَمِمَّا تَعْبُدُونَ مِن دُونِ ٱللَّهِ كَفَرْنَا بِكُمْ$$
$$وَبَدَا بَيْنَنَا وَبَيْنَكُمُ ٱلْعَدَاوَةُ وَٱلْبَغْضَاءُ أَبَدًا حَتَّىٰ تُؤْمِنُوا۟ بِٱللَّهِ$$

---

[1] عقيدة

[2] سيرة

[3] saw - *sal-lal-laahu-'alihi-wa-sallam* (صلى الله عليه وسلم) means "Peace be upon Prophet Muhammad."

[4] Known as Abraham in Western literature

[5] *alaihis salaam* means "peace be upon him" which is used for prophets.

وَحْدَهُ إِلَّا قَوْلَ إِبْرَاهِيمَ لِأَبِيهِ لَأَسْتَغْفِرَنَّ لَكَ وَمَآ أَمْلِكُ لَكَ مِنَ اللَّهِ مِن شَىْءٍ رَّبَّنَا عَلَيْكَ تَوَكَّلْنَا وَإِلَيْكَ أَنَبْنَا وَإِلَيْكَ ٱلْمَصِيرُ

> There is for you an excellent example (to follow) in Ibrahim and those with him, when they said to their people: "We are clear of you and of whatever you worship besides Allah. We have rejected you, and there has arisen, between us and you, enmity and hatred forever unless you believe in Allah and Him alone" except when Ibrahim said to his father: "I will pray for your forgiveness though I have no power to get it on your behalf from Allah[6]." (They prayed): "Our Lord! In You do we trust and to You do we turn in repentance and to You is our final return. [Al-Mumtahinah, 60:4]

How decisive and critical is the declaration of correct *'aqeedah*? The strongest indication comes in the timing of the revelation of the Quranic chapter *Al-Kafirun* (Chapter No. 109).

Given the hostile condition of Makkah in the early days of Islam, common sense suggested that nothing should be done to further aggravate the enmity between Muslims and non-Muslims and any proclamation which could intensify the hostility against Muslims should be postponed until Muslims gained strength and conditions became more favorable. But Allah, by revealing the following verses, commanded Prophet Muhammad (saw) to proclaim *Tawheed*[7] (oneness of Allah) with full force in that very adverse condition:

قُلْ يَٰٓأَيُّهَا ٱلْكَٰفِرُونَ (1) لَآ أَعْبُدُ مَا تَعْبُدُونَ (2) وَلَآ أَنتُمْ عَٰبِدُونَ مَآ أَعْبُدُ (3) وَلَآ أَنَا عَابِدٌ مَّا عَبَدتُّمْ (4) وَلَآ أَنتُمْ عَٰبِدُونَ مَآ أَعْبُدُ (5) لَكُمْ دِينُكُمْ وَلِىَ دِينِ (6)

> Say, "O disbelievers! I do not worship what you worship. Nor are you worshippers of what I worship. Nor will I be a worshipper of what you worship. Nor will you be worshippers of what I worship. For you is your religion, and for me is my religion." [Al-Kafirun, 109:1-6]

---

[6] There may be a question: Why did Prophet Ibrahim promise his idol worshipping father that he would pray for his forgiveness? The answer to this question comes in the Quranic verse At-Taubah [9:113-114],

[7] توحيد

Since *'aqeedah* plays the pivotal role in Islam and the entire structure of Islam hinges upon correct *'aqeedah*, it is extremely important to fully and correctly understand it – this is what this book attempts to explain to its readers.

Chapter 1 - *Tawheed*

Man is constantly surrounded by needs which know no limit. Both his physical and spiritual demands are boundless. He is by nature greedy and insatiable. Thus he cannot rely upon someone whose power, wealth and knowledge is finite and limited.

Man by nature is more fragile than glass and flimsier than a bubble. He is dependent upon hundreds of objects for his existence. There are thousands of objects which are his enemy. He can be protected only by the One who has full control over the universe; controls every atom of it; determines the property and ability of every object; can cease or change the nature of any object; is the Creator of everything; is the Sustainer of everything; never suffers from any deficiency or weakness; is holding the entire universe in perfect balance; is all-knowing; is always alert; and is never overtaken by sleep.

Creations are countless and their needs are unlimited. Some of their needs are so subtle that even the creations themselves do not know about them. They are feeble and helpless like a newly born baby. They need the affection and attention of a deity who is more loving and caring than a mother. That deity ought to be kind as well as wise – attributes necessary for being a true guardian, mentor and caretaker.

A close examination of the universe and its intricacies reveals that no one other than Allah can be in full control of the universe, as Allah Himself has mentioned in the Holy Quran:

$$\text{سَنُرِيهِمْ ءَايَـٰتِنَا فِى ٱلْأَفَاقِ وَفِىٓ أَنفُسِهِمْ حَتَّىٰ يَتَبَيَّنَ لَهُمْ أَنَّهُ}$$
$$\text{ٱلْحَقُّ أَوَلَمْ يَكْفِ بِرَبِّكَ أَنَّهُۥ عَلَىٰ كُلِّ شَىْءٍ شَهِيدٌ}$$

> Soon We will show them our signs in the (furthest) regions (of the earth), and in their own souls, until it becomes manifest to them that this is the Truth. Is it not enough that your Lord is witness to all things? [Fussilat, 41:53]

Indeed there is no one worthy of worship except the Almighty Allah.

Deception and Ignorance

In this world, the apparent system of cause and effect is so engrained that a man is often deceived in recognizing the real source of loss and benefit. As a result, he often elevates a weak and feeble object like himself as a deity and lives with this deception for his entire life.

Man eats, drinks, bears children, acquires knowledge of the skies and conquers oceans and deserts. But if he does not recognize his Creator, there can be no ignorance greater than this. A person knows who his father is, but does not know who created him, his father, his forefathers, the universe, the earth, the sky, mountains and gardens; he does not know who provides sustenance, who determines destiny and who gives life and death.

If a person does not know the Hindi language, he is considered illiterate in the Hindi-speaking circle; if he does not know the Urdu language, he is considered illiterate in the Urdu-speaking circle; if he does not know the Arabic language, he is considered illiterate in the Arabic-speaking circle. What about the person who does not know who his Creator is and whom he should worship? There can be no ignorance greater than this.

Divine Knowledge

Divine knowledge - the knowledge of Allah, His attributes, His commandments and the Life Hereafter - is the most important and highest form of knowledge. This knowledge is beyond the reach, capacity and experience of human beings. The only source of this knowledge is the group of prophets.

Allah is unique. He is above any comparison or imagination. A human mind with the faculty which he uses to reason and think about material objects cannot imagine and comprehend Allah. Human intelligence and wisdom is of no use in this endeavor because this is an arena where human imagination and speculation lead nowhere.

Divine knowledge is critical for the success and welfare of mankind. It plays a key role in forming belief and character of individuals and society. It enables a person to know his worth and reality. It allows him to understand the intricacies of the universe and secrets of life. It helps him determine his real position and status in this world. It guides him in maintaining amicable relationships with fellow human beings. It enables him to determine the direction and purpose of his life with confidence and conviction.

Divine knowledge has been regarded as the highest form of knowledge by every nation in every era of human civilization; it inspires and engages every individual who is thoughtful and serious about life and its consequences. Ignorance, intentional or unintentional, of divine knowledge leads to failure and destruction of immeasurable magnitude.

Prophets

Prophets were the chosen individuals who were enlightened by Allah with divine knowledge. They served as the medium between Allah and people. They were blessed with true understanding of who Allah is, what His attributes are and what He expects from human beings. They were bestowed with the highest form of *iman*[1] (faith) and *noor* (enlightenment), as has been mentioned in the following verses of the Holy Quran:

$$وَكَذَٰلِكَ نُرِىٓ إِبْرَٰهِيمَ مَلَكُوتَ ٱلسَّمَٰوَٰتِ وَٱلْأَرْضِ وَلِيَكُونَ مِنَ ٱلْمُوقِنِينَ$$

Thus We showed to Ibrahim the visible and invisible world of the heavens and the earth so that he could be among those who believe [Al-An'am, 6:75]

$$أَتُحَٰٓجُّونِّى فِى ٱللَّهِ وَقَدْ هَدَٰنِ$$

Do you argue with me about God? He has already guided me.[2] [Al-An'am, 6:80]

Mission of Prophets

The first and foremost mission of all the prophets was to introduce and propagate correct *'aqeedah* about Allah; to develop correct relationship between Allah and man; and to teach man how to obey and worship Allah. They taught that Allah is the only source of gain and loss, He is the only one who deserves to be worshipped, He is the only one worthy of

---

[1] ایمان

[2] This was the response of Prophet Ibrahim to his nation when they argued with him about the attributes of Allah.

supplication and He is the only one who deserves our full attention and devotion.

Prophets also worked tirelessly to fight and eradicate *shirk*[3] (polytheism) which people used to practice in many different forms. People believed in Allah, but they also believed that Allah has appointed idols, ghosts and seers (living or dead) as His deputies in the same way as a king appoints deputies for different regions of his kingdom to govern and look after the affairs of his subjects. They worshipped those objects believing that they were elevated to their revered position by Allah and were granted special power and privilege to intercede on their behalf in the court of Allah.

To a serious reader of the Holy Quran, it becomes immediately clear that the common objective of all the prophets was to fight *shirk* and idol worshipping and eradicate vices from the society. The Holy Quran mentions it sometimes briefly and sometimes in detail, as in the following verses:

وَمَآ أَرْسَلْنَا مِن قَبْلِكَ مِن رَّسُولٍ إِلَّا نُوحِىٓ إِلَيْهِ أَنَّهُ لَا إِلَـٰهَ إِلَّا أَنَا۠ فَٱعْبُدُونِ

We did not send before you any messenger but We revealed to him that there is no god but Me, so worship Me." [Al-Anbiya, 21:25]

وَٱلْوَزْنُ يَوْمَئِذٍ ٱلْحَقُّ فَمَن ثَقُلَتْ مَوَٰزِينُهُ فَأُو۟لَـٰٓئِكَ هُمُ ٱلْمُفْلِحُونَ (8) وَمَنْ خَفَّتْ مَوَٰزِينُهُ فَأُو۟لَـٰٓئِكَ ٱلَّذِينَ خَسِرُوٓا۟ أَنفُسَهُم بِمَا كَانُوا۟ بِـَٔايَـٰتِنَا يَظْلِمُونَ (9) وَلَقَدْ مَكَّنَّـٰكُمْ فِى ٱلْأَرْضِ وَجَعَلْنَا لَكُمْ فِيهَا مَعَـٰيِشَ قَلِيلًا مَّا تَشْكُرُونَ (10) وَلَقَدْ خَلَقْنَـٰكُمْ ثُمَّ صَوَّرْنَـٰكُمْ ثُمَّ قُلْنَا لِلْمَلَـٰٓئِكَةِ ٱسْجُدُوا۟ لِءَادَمَ فَسَجَدُوٓا۟ إِلَّا إِبْلِيسَ لَمْ يَكُن مِّنَ ٱلسَّـٰجِدِينَ (11) قَالَ مَا مَنَعَكَ أَلَّا تَسْجُدَ إِذْ أَمَرْتُكَ قَالَ أَنَا۠ خَيْرٌ مِّنْهُ خَلَقْتَنِى مِن نَّارٍ وَخَلَقْتَهُ مِن طِينٍ (12)

The Weighing (of deeds) on that day is definite. As for those whose scales are heavy, they will be the successful ones. But those whose scales are light, they are the ones who have brought loss to themselves, because they did not do justice to Our signs. We established you on the earth,

---

شرك [3]

and created in it means of living for you. Little did you appreciate. We created you, then gave you a shape, then We said to the angels, "Prostrate before Adam." So, they all prostrated except Iblis; he did not join those who fell prostrate. Allah said, "What has prevented you from prostrating when I ordered you?" He said, "I am better than him. You have created me of fire and created him of clay." [Al-A'raf, 7:8-12]

وَأَنِ ٱسْتَغْفِرُواْ رَبَّكُمْ ثُمَّ تُوبُوٓاْ إِلَيْهِ يُمَتِّعْكُم مَّتَـٰعًا حَسَنًا إِلَىٰٓ أَجَلٍ مُّسَمًّى وَيُؤْتِ كُلَّ ذِى فَضْلٍ فَضْلَهُۥ ۖ وَإِن تَوَلَّوْاْ فَإِنِّىٓ أَخَافُ عَلَيْكُمْ عَذَابَ يَوْمٍ كَبِيرٍ (3) إِلَى ٱللَّهِ مَرْجِعُكُمْ ۖ وَهُوَ عَلَىٰ كُلِّ شَىْءٍ قَدِيرٌ (4) أَلَآ إِنَّهُمْ يَثْنُونَ صُدُورَهُمْ لِيَسْتَخْفُواْ مِنْهُ ۚ أَلَا حِينَ يَسْتَغْشُونَ ثِيَابَهُمْ يَعْلَمُ مَا يُسِرُّونَ وَمَا يُعْلِنُونَ ۚ إِنَّهُۥ عَلِيمٌ بِذَاتِ ٱلصُّدُورِ (5) وَمَا مِن دَآبَّةٍ فِى ٱلْأَرْضِ إِلَّا عَلَى ٱللَّهِ رِزْقُهَا وَيَعْلَمُ مُسْتَقَرَّهَا وَمُسْتَوْدَعَهَا ۚ كُلٌّ فِى كِتَٰبٍ مُّبِينٍ (6) وَهُوَ ٱلَّذِى خَلَقَ ٱلسَّمَٰوَٰتِ وَٱلْأَرْضَ فِى سِتَّةِ أَيَّامٍ وَكَانَ عَرْشُهُۥ عَلَى ٱلْمَآءِ لِيَبْلُوَكُمْ أَيُّكُمْ أَحْسَنُ عَمَلًا ۗ وَلَئِن قُلْتَ إِنَّكُم مَّبْعُوثُونَ مِنۢ بَعْدِ ٱلْمَوْتِ لَيَقُولَنَّ ٱلَّذِينَ كَفَرُوٓاْ إِنْ هَٰذَآ إِلَّا سِحْرٌ مُّبِينٌ (7) وَلَئِنْ أَخَّرْنَا عَنْهُمُ ٱلْعَذَابَ إِلَىٰٓ أُمَّةٍ مَّعْدُودَةٍ لَّيَقُولُنَّ مَا يَحْبِسُهُۥٓ ۗ أَلَا يَوْمَ يَأْتِيهِمْ لَيْسَ مَصْرُوفًا عَنْهُمْ وَحَاقَ بِهِم مَّا كَانُواْ بِهِۦ يَسْتَهْزِءُونَ (8)

And you must seek forgiveness from your Lord, then, turn to Him in repentance, and He will provide you with good things to enjoy for a given time, and bestow His extra favor on everyone who has extra good deeds (in his account). And if you turn away, then, I fear for you the punishment of a terrible day. To Allah is your return, and He is powerful over everything." Beware! They bend their chests to hide from Him. Beware! When they cover up themselves with their clothes, He knows what they hide and what they expose. Surely, He is all aware of what lies in the hearts. There is no creature on the earth whose sustenance is not undertaken by Allah. He knows its permanent and temporary place. Everything is in a clear book. He is the One who created the heavens and the earth in six days, while His throne was on water, so that He might test you as to who among you is better in deed. And if you say: "You shall be raised after death," the disbelievers will surely say, "This is nothing but sheer magic." And if We defer the punishment for them for a certain time, they will say, "What is holding it back?" Beware! The day it will visit them, it shall not be turned back from them, and they shall be besieged by what they used to ridicule. [Hud, 11:3-8]

The very first invitation that prophets gave to their people was:

إِلَىٰ قَوْمِهِ فَقَالَ يَـٰقَوْمِ ٱعْبُدُواْ ٱللَّهَ مَا لَكُم مِّنْ إِلَـٰهٍ غَيْرُهُ

"O my people! Worship Allah. You have no deity other than Him." [Al-A'raf, 7:59]

They worked hard to nurture strong and close relationship between Allah and people, as has been mentioned in the Holy Quran:

وَمَآ أُمِرُوٓاْ إِلَّا لِيَعْبُدُواْ ٱللَّهَ مُخْلِصِينَ لَهُ ٱلدِّينَ حُنَفَآءَ

And they have been commanded no more than this: To worship Allah, offering Him sincere devotion, being true (in faith). [Al-Baiyinah, 98:5]

There should not remain any unfamiliarity and distance between Allah and His servants. The object of a person's love, worship, devotion, submission, obedience, sacrifice, supplication, struggle, fear, hope and entreaty should become Allah. His heart and mind should become fully directed towards Allah, as has been mentioned in the Holy Quran:

قُلْ إِنَّ صَلَاتِى وَنُسُكِى وَمَحْيَاىَ وَمَمَاتِى لِلَّهِ رَبِّ ٱلْعَـٰلَمِينَ (162) لَا شَرِيكَ لَهُ ۖ وَبِذَٰلِكَ أُمِرْتُ وَأَنَا۠ أَوَّلُ ٱلْمُسْلِمِينَ (163)

Say, "My prayer, my offering, my life and my death are for Allah, the Lord of all the worlds. For Him there is no partner. And thus I have been commanded, and I am the first one to submit." [Al-An'am, 6:162-163]

Prophets were successful in directing people towards Allah. People shunned the life of disobedience, adopted the life of obedience and became free from the slavery to fellow human beings. But ignorance persisted and polytheistic beliefs kept on sprouting in the hearts and minds of people. Even those who had been faithfully following their prophet slowly started deviating from the true path after the prophet passed away, as the Holy Quran mentions:

$$\text{وَمَا يُؤْمِنُ أَكْثَرُهُم بِٱللَّهِ إِلَّا وَهُم مُّشْرِكُونَ}$$

And most of them believe not in Allah without associating (other as partners) with Him! [Yusuf, 12:106]

They continued drifting away from Allah and getting closer to their imagined gods, as the Holy Quran mentions:

$$\text{وَمِنَ ٱلنَّاسِ مَن يَتَّخِذُ مِن دُونِ ٱللَّهِ أَندَادًا يُحِبُّونَهُمْ كَحُبِّ ٱللَّهِ}$$

Yet there are men who take (for worship) others besides Allah, as equal (with Allah). They love them as they should love Allah. [Al-Baqarah, 2:165]

$$\text{وَإِذَا ذُكِرَ ٱللَّهُ وَحْدَهُ ٱشْمَأَزَّتْ قُلُوبُ ٱلَّذِينَ لَا يُؤْمِنُونَ بِٱلْآخِرَةِ}$$
$$\text{وَإِذَا ذُكِرَ ٱلَّذِينَ مِن دُونِهِ إِذَا هُمْ يَسْتَبْشِرُونَ}$$

When Allah, the One and Only One, is mentioned, the hearts of those who do not believe in the Hereafter are filled with disgust and horror, but when (gods) other than Him are mentioned, behold, they are filled with joy! [Az-Zumar, 39:45]

Prophets' Method of Inviting People towards Allah and the Life Hereafter

Prophets utilized two strategies to convey divine knowledge to people and clear their misconceptions.

1. They persistently explained the attributes of Allah with absolute clarity, as no other strategy is more effective in dispelling ignorance and *shirk* than this. Ignorance and *shirk* are the main

reasons for why people become forgetful about Allah, His attributes and His commandments and start worshipping other gods, as the Holy Quran mentions:

$$\text{وَمَا قَدَرُواْ ٱللَّهَ حَقَّ قَدْرِهِ وَٱلْأَرْضُ جَمِيعًا قَبْضَتُهُ يَوْمَ ٱلْقِيَـٰمَةِ وَٱلسَّمَـٰوَٰتُ مَطْوِيَّـٰتٌ بِيَمِينِهِ سُبْحَـٰنَهُ وَتَعَـٰلَىٰ عَمَّا يُشْرِكُونَ}$$

> They do not esteem Allah as is rightly due to Him. The whole earth would be a fistful of His on the Day of Resurrection, and the heavens would be rolled up in His right hand. Too immaculate is He and too high for what they associate with Him! [Az-Zumar, 39:67]

2. They explained the reality of creations and removed the veil of deception from the eyes of people. They explained how feeble all the creations are; how impotent they are in harming or benefiting anyone; how helpless they are in helping anyone; how undeserving they are for being worshipped and how untrustworthy they are to depend upon.

Prophets described the attributes of Allah in such an effective manner that they completely transformed the hearts and minds of people. For example, they explained the attribute *as-Samad* as: Every atom of the universe is completely dependent upon Allah, whereas Allah is completely independent of everything.

They explained that Allah is running the entire universe all by Himself and it is His control under which all the skies and earth are functioning. The following verses of the Holy Quran testify to this effect:

$$\text{أَلَا لَهُ ٱلْخَلْقُ وَٱلْأَمْرُ}$$

> Lo! To Him alone belong the creation and the command. [Al-A'raf, 7:54]

$$\text{يُدَبِّرُ ٱلْأَمْرَ مِنَ ٱلسَّمَآءِ إِلَى ٱلْأَرْضِ}$$

> He governs everything from the heaven to the earth. [As-Sajdah, 32:5]

وَقُلِ ٱلْحَمْدُ لِلَّهِ ٱلَّذِى لَمْ يَتَّخِذْ وَلَدًا وَلَمْ يَكُن لَّهُ شَرِيكٌ فِى ٱلْمُلْكِ وَلَمْ يَكُن لَّهُ وَلِىٌّ مِّنَ ٱلذُّلِّ وَكَبِّرْهُ تَكْبِيرًا

And say: "All praise be to Allah Who has neither taken to Himself a son, nor has He any partner in His kingdom, nor does He need anyone, out of weakness, to protect Him." So glorify Him in a manner worthy of His glory. [Al-Isra, 17:111]

لَا يَمْلِكُونَ مِثْقَالَ ذَرَّةٍ فِى ٱلسَّمَٰوَٰتِ وَلَا فِى ٱلْأَرْضِ وَمَا لَهُمْ فِيهِمَا مِن شِرْكٍ وَمَا لَهُ مِنْهُم مِّن ظَهِيرٍ

They own not even the smallest particle, neither in the heavens nor on the earth; nor do they have any share in the ownership of either of them. Nor is anyone of them a helper of Allah. [Saba, 34:22]

وَلِلَّهِ خَزَائِنُ ٱلسَّمَٰوَٰتِ وَٱلْأَرْضِ

The treasures of the heavens and the earth belong to Allah. [Al-Munafiqun, 63:7]

يَدَاهُ مَبْسُوطَتَانِ يُنفِقُ كَيْفَ يَشَآءُ

No! His both hands are wide open. He spends as He wills. [Al-Maidah, 5:64]

يَرْزُقُ مَن يَشَآءُ بِغَيْرِ حِسَابٍ

Allah has full authority and power to bestow provision without measure on anyone He wills. [Al-Baqara, 2:212]

Allah is the only one who can fulfill the desires of a greedy person. He is the only one who knows what is hidden and what is open. He is everywhere and all-knowing, as is mentioned in the Holy Quran.

عَٰلِمُ ٱلْغَيْبِ وَٱلشَّهَٰدَةِ

He knows the unseen as well as that which is open. [Al-An'am, 6:73]

يَعْلَمُ خَائِنَةَ ٱلْأَعْيُنِ وَمَا تُخْفِى ٱلصُّدُورُ

He knows even the most secret glance of the eyes and all the secrets that hearts conceal. [Ghafir, 40:19]

Thus His is the only knowledge that can be trusted. He knows the desires that are hidden in the hearts and even those which the bearer does not recognize. He is the one who fulfills all wishes. He is the Protector of man for whose protection He has appointed guards.

لَهُ مُعَقِّبَٰتٌ مِّنۢ بَيْنِ يَدَيْهِ وَمِنْ خَلْفِهِ يَحْفَظُونَهُ مِنْ أَمْرِ ٱللَّهِ

There are guardians over everyone, both in front of him and behind him, who guard him by Allah's command. [Ar-R'ad, 13:11]

Allah is unique. He is nearer to you than whoever is your nearest. He is nearer to you than your jugular vein. To a dying person, He is nearer than those who are tending to him.

وَنَحْنُ أَقْرَبُ إِلَيْهِ مِنْ حَبْلِ ٱلْوَرِيدِ

We are nearer to him than (his) jugular vein. [Qaf, 50:16]

وَنَحْنُ أَقْرَبُ إِلَيْهِ مِنكُمْ وَلَٰكِن لَّا تُبْصِرُونَ

But We are nearer to him than you, but you cannot see. [Al-Waqi'ah, 56:85]

He listens to the prayer and supplication of everyone at every place. There is no barrier between Him and His slave. Nor is the mediation of someone needed to forward the entreaty to Him.

وَإِذَا سَأَلَكَ عِبَادِى عَنِّى فَإِنِّى قَرِيبٌ أُجِيبُ دَعْوَةَ ٱلدَّاعِ إِذَا دَعَانِ فَلْيَسْتَجِيبُوا۟ لِى وَلْيُؤْمِنُوا۟ بِى لَعَلَّهُمْ يَرْشُدُونَ

When My servants ask you about Me, then (tell them that) I am indeed near (to them). I respond to the call of everyone when he calls on Me. So they should respond to Me and have faith in Me so that they may be on the right path. [Al-Baqarah, 2:186]

Allah's love and mercy is beyond imagination. Parents' love and affection for their children is merely a reflection of Allah's love and affection. He is always alert and awake. He is in full control of every atom of the universe. That is why He is never negligent or forgetful.

اَللَّهُ لَا إِلَـٰهَ إِلَّا هُوَ ٱلْحَىُّ ٱلْقَيُّومُ لَا تَأْخُذُهُ سِنَةٌ وَلَا نَوْمٌ

Allah! There is no god but He, the Living, the Self-subsisting, Eternal. No slumber can seize Him nor any sleep. [Al-Baqarah, 2:255]

Prophets explained that the creations do not possess qualities of the Creator and they are absolutely weak, needy, helpless and dependent, as is mentioned in the following verses of the Holy Quran:

لَهُ دَعْوَةُ ٱلْحَقِّ وَٱلَّذِينَ يَدْعُونَ مِن دُونِهِ لَا يَسْتَجِيبُونَ لَهُم بِشَىْءٍ إِلَّا كَبَـٰسِطِ كَفَّيْهِ إِلَى ٱلْمَآءِ لِيَبْلُغَ فَاهُ وَمَا هُوَ بِبَـٰلِغِهِ وَمَا دُعَآءُ ٱلْكَـٰفِرِينَ إِلَّا فِى ضَلَـٰلٍ

True prayers are to be directed to Him alone; and those to whom they pray instead of Him do not respond to them at all, but they are like the ones who stretch their hands towards water so that it may reach their mouth (by itself), while it is not to reach them. And the prayer of the disbelievers (that they make to false gods) is nothing but straying in void. [Ar-R'ad, 13:14]

يَـٰٓأَيُّهَا ٱلنَّاسُ ضُرِبَ مَثَلٌ فَٱسْتَمِعُواْ لَهُ إِنَّ ٱلَّذِينَ تَدْعُونَ مِن دُونِ ٱللَّهِ لَن يَخْلُقُواْ ذُبَابًا وَلَوِ ٱجْتَمَعُواْ لَهُ وَإِن يَسْلُبْهُمُ ٱلذُّبَابُ شَيْئًا لَّا يَسْتَنقِذُوهُ مِنْهُ ضَعُفَ ٱلطَّالِبُ وَٱلْمَطْلُوبُ (73) مَا قَدَرُواْ ٱللَّهَ حَقَّ قَدْرِهِ إِنَّ ٱللَّهَ لَقَوِىٌّ عَزِيزٌ (74)

O men! Here is a parable set forth! Listen to it! Those on whom, besides Allah, you call, cannot create (even) a fly, if they all joined together for the purpose! And if the fly should snatch away anything from them, they would have no power to release it from the fly. Feeble are those who petition and those to whom they petition! No just estimate have they made of Allah, for Allah is He Who is strong and able to carry out His Will. [Al-Hajj, 22:73-74]

مَثَلُ ٱلَّذِينَ ٱتَّخَذُواْ مِن دُونِ ٱللَّهِ أَوْلِيَآءَ كَمَثَلِ ٱلْعَنكَبُوتِ ٱتَّخَذَتْ بَيْتًا ۖ وَإِنَّ أَوْهَنَ ٱلْبُيُوتِ لَبَيْتُ ٱلْعَنكَبُوتِ ۘ لَوْ كَانُواْ يَعْلَمُونَ

The parable of those who take protectors other than Allah is that of the spider, who builds (to itself) a house; but truly the flimsiest of houses is the spider's house if they but knew. [Al-Ankabut, 29:41]

يُولِجُ ٱلَّيْلَ فِى ٱلنَّهَارِ وَيُولِجُ ٱلنَّهَارَ فِى ٱلَّيْلِ وَسَخَّرَ ٱلشَّمْسَ وَٱلْقَمَرَ كُلٌّ يَجْرِى لِأَجَلٍ مُّسَمًّى ۚ ذَٰلِكُمُ ٱللَّهُ رَبُّكُمْ لَهُ ٱلْمُلْكُ وَٱلَّذِينَ تَدْعُونَ مِن دُونِهِ مَا يَمْلِكُونَ مِن قِطْمِيرٍ (13) إِن تَدْعُوهُمْ لَا يَسْمَعُواْ دُعَآءَكُمْ وَلَوْ سَمِعُواْ مَا ٱسْتَجَابُواْ لَكُمْ ۖ وَيَوْمَ ٱلْقِيَٰمَةِ يَكْفُرُونَ بِشِرْكِكُمْ ۚ وَلَا يُنَبِّئُكَ مِثْلُ خَبِيرٍ (14) يَٰٓأَيُّهَا ٱلنَّاسُ أَنتُمُ ٱلْفُقَرَآءُ إِلَى ٱللَّهِ ۖ وَٱللَّهُ هُوَ ٱلْغَنِىُّ ٱلْحَمِيدُ (15)

He makes night run into day, day run into night, and has harnessed the sun and the moon so that each runs in its determined course. This is Allah your Lord; His is the kingdom; and those you invoke apart from Him are not masters even of the skin on a date-palm stone. You pray to them, but they do not hear your call; and even if they heard you, they could not answer your prayer; and on the Day of Resurrection they will deny that you worshipped them. None can acquaint you (with the reality) as He who is informed of everything. O men! It is you who stand in need of Allah. As for Allah, He is above all need, worthy of praise. [Fatir, 35:13-15]

وَٱتَّخَذُواْ مِن دُونِهِ ءَالِهَةً لَّا يَخْلُقُونَ شَيْئًا وَهُمْ يُخْلَقُونَ وَلَا يَمْلِكُونَ لِأَنفُسِهِمْ ضَرًّا وَلَا نَفْعًا وَلَا يَمْلِكُونَ مَوْتًا وَلَا حَيَٰوةً وَلَا نُشُورًا

Yet they choose apart from Him gods who have not created anything and have themselves been created, who possess no power over their loss or gain, or their death or life or being raised to life again. [Al-Furqan, 25:3]

Two Categories of People

As a result of the preaching of prophets, two groups of people emerged.

1. One group consisted of those who accepted prophets' call and started the journey of life in the light of divine revelation which prophets had received from Allah. They lived a life of piety, spirituality and good manners. They utilized their faculty of thinking and reasoning in the right direction and with due diligence. They intimately experienced the truthfulness of the teachings of prophets and their *iman* and *yaqeen*[4] (conviction) increased day by day, as has been mentioned in the Holy Quran:

$$\text{وَمَا زَادَهُمْ إِلَّآ إِيمَـٰنًا وَتَسْلِيمًا}$$

   And this enhanced their faith and obedience. [Al-Ahzab, 33:22]

2. The other group consisted of those who relied solely on their intellect, reasoning and know-how. In order to study and analyze the existence and attributes of Allah, they employed the same techniques and methods which they had utilized in their laboratories to study and analyze a plant or a physical phenomenon. As a result, they reached reckless and irrational conclusions about Allah – what He is and what He is not. The conclusions suggesting "Allah is not like this" far outnumbered the conclusions suggesting "Allah is like this".

When a person is deprived of the light of *iman*, he is more inclined to rely on negatives than on positives. This is the primary reason for why the Greek philosophers focused more on negatives than on positives while discussing the Supreme Being and His attributes. And it remains a fact that any system, religion or way of life that is founded on negatives cannot survive for long.

Sheikh-ul Islam Ibn Taimiyah (d. 1328) said, "Greek philosophers, while talking about Allah, took great pains to focus on the attributes that they considered unfitting for Him, but described only minimally the attributes

---

[4] يقين

that they thought were appropriate for Him." That is why Greek philosophy puts greater emphasis on what Allah is not than on what He is.

Contrary to that, the Holy Quran focuses more on describing who Allah is and very little on what He is not. The same is true for other divine scriptures as well. The Holy Quran says:

هُوَ ٱللَّهُ ٱلَّذِى لَا إِلَٰهَ إِلَّا هُوَ عَٰلِمُ ٱلْغَيْبِ وَٱلشَّهَٰدَةِ هُوَ ٱلرَّحْمَٰنُ ٱلرَّحِيمُ (22) هُوَ ٱللَّهُ ٱلَّذِى لَا إِلَٰهَ إِلَّا هُوَ ٱلْمَلِكُ ٱلْقُدُّوسُ ٱلسَّلَٰمُ ٱلْمُؤْمِنُ ٱلْمُهَيْمِنُ ٱلْعَزِيزُ ٱلْجَبَّارُ ٱلْمُتَكَبِّرُ سُبْحَٰنَ ٱللَّهِ عَمَّا يُشْرِكُونَ (23) هُوَ ٱللَّهُ ٱلْخَٰلِقُ ٱلْبَارِئُ ٱلْمُصَوِّرُ لَهُ ٱلْأَسْمَآءُ ٱلْحُسْنَىٰ يُسَبِّحُ لَهُ مَا فِى ٱلسَّمَٰوَٰتِ وَٱلْأَرْضِ وَهُوَ ٱلْعَزِيزُ ٱلْحَكِيمُ (24)

He is Allah, other than whom there is no deity, Knower of the unseen and the seen. He is the Most Gracious, Most Merciful. He is Allah, other than whom there is no deity, the Sovereign, the Pure, the Perfect, the Guardian of Faith, the Overseer, the Exalted in Might, the Compeller and the Superior. Exalted is Allah above whatever they associate with Him. He is Allah, the Creator, the Inventor and the Fashioner. To Him belong the best names. Whatever is in the heavens and earth is glorifying Him. And He is the Exalted in Might, the Wise. [Al-Hashr, 59:22-24]

لَيْسَ كَمِثْلِهِ شَىْءٌ وَهُوَ ٱلسَّمِيعُ ٱلْبَصِيرُ

Nothing is like Him. And He is the All-Hearing, the All-Seeing. [Ash-Shura, 42:11]

Ibn Taimiyah further said, "Negatives, even though they may be in the hundreds, do not have the same effect as that of a single positive." The history of mankind bears ample testimony to this fact. Human life derives energy, sustenance and inspiration from positives; the role of negatives is very little.

Customs and Rituals of *Shirk*

After the core tenets of *Tawheed* have been enumerated, it is also necessary to point out the customs and rituals of *shirk* and the diseases and vices that have proliferated among Muslims due to ignorance, lack of proper knowledge of the Holy Quran and *sunnah*[5] (sayings and practices of Prophet Muhammad), and the influence of an un-Islamic environment.

Omnipresence (being everywhere), Omniscience (knowing everything) and Omnipotence (having unlimited power and authority) are exclusive attributes of Allah. To engage in acts of worship - such as bowing down in front of someone; fasting to please someone; traveling long distances to visit shrines and treating those shrines as *Baitullah*[6]; sacrificing animals on shrines; making votive offerings; and taking devotional vows - are rituals and practices of *shirk*.

There are certain forms of worship and veneration that are suitable only for Allah and not for anyone else. Knowledge of *ghaib*[7] (unseen) is the domain of Allah and is beyond human reach. No one except Allah knows the secrets of hearts, thoughts of minds and purpose of intention.

One should not imagine Allah to be like a king or monarch of the world. Allah does not need the assistance of advisors, ministers or courtiers. No type of prostration is allowed in front of anyone except Allah.

The rituals of *hajj*[8] (pilgrimage to Makkah) and display of utmost reverence for *Baitullah* and *Haram* (area surrounding *Baitullah*) are exclusive and do not apply to any other place or structure.

To revere pious and saintly people in a manner that is only fitting for Allah is forbidden. To devote and sacrifice animals in the name of pious and saintly people is forbidden. It is only the right of Allah that an animal be sacrificed in His name. It is an act of *shirk* to believe in astrology and in the influence of stars on the affairs of the worlds. It is an act of *shirk* to believe in astrologers, soothsayers and fortune-tellers.

---

[5] سنة

[6] *Baitullah* is the cube-shaped structure in Makkah which is known as the House of Allah

[7] غيب

[8] حج

One should also be cognizant of *Tawheed* while choosing names for children. The names that are misleading or have any connotation of *shirk* should be avoided. No vow should be taken except in the name of Allah. Sacrificial animals should not be slaughtered at a venue which has been a place of idol-worshipping or related festivals.

In revering and adoring Prophet Muhammad (saw), proper balance must be maintained and limits must not be crossed as the Christians have done for Prophet Isa[9] (*alaihis salaam*). Keeping and revering images and pictures of pious people and saints must be completely avoided.

Consequences of Shirk and Idol Worshipping

The practices of *shirk* and idol worshipping are the most horrific and deadliest form of ignorance. These practices have thrived in all ages and in all nations regardless of their political, economic and social condition. It is the sin that ignites the anger of Allah the most. It is the greatest obstacle that prevents humans from making spiritual and moral advancements. It is the vice that makes people fall from heights of dignity into pits of shame and disgrace.

Countering such beliefs and practices was the mission of all the prophets and will remain the primary mission of all the rightly guided reformers until the Last Day, as the Holy Quran has mentioned:

$$وَجَعَلَهَا كَلِمَةً بَاقِيَةً فِى عَقِبِهِ لَعَلَّهُمْ يَرْجِعُونَ$$

And he made it a word remaining among his descendants
that they might return to Allah. [Az-Zukhruf, 43:28]

Shirk should not be taken lightly. It should not be ignored in the face of new challenges and demands of modern time. It should not be treated like defiance of a political ordinance or man-made legislation; its consequences are far reaching and very devastating. It should not be given lower priority among the objectives of *d'awah*[10] (calling towards Allah and His religion) and *tabligh*[11] (propagation of Allah's religion).

---

[9] Known as Jesus in Western literature

[10] دعوة

[11] تبليغ

Shirk should not be thought of as a thing of the dark ages with no attraction for the people of modern age. It is mistake to assume that it was fascinating only to the people of uncivilized ages and has no attraction for the people of today. It still continues to emerge in many different shapes and colors. Many nations and countries are still practicing it openly (in the form of idol worshipping) and even many Muslim are indulged in it. What the Holy Quran has declared in the following verse still holds true

$$وَمَا يُؤْمِنُ أَكْثَرُهُم بِٱللَّهِ إِلَّا وَهُم مُّشْرِكُونَ$$

And most of them do not believe in Allah without associating partners with Him. [Yusuf, 12:106]

If there was anyone who could have been spared the consequences of wrong *'aqeedah* (i.e. *shirk*), it would have been the Prophet's uncle Abu Talib who was the most formidable protector of the Prophet (saw). All the biographers of the Prophet (saw) agree that Abu Talib was like a shield between the Prophet and the enemies of Islam, and he risked his own life and prestige in protecting the Prophet. Yet, when he was on his deathbed and Abu Jahl and Abdullah bin Abi Ummayah were sitting by his side, the Prophet (saw) came to him and said, "O Uncle! Recite the Kalimah *La Ila-hu Il-lallah*[12] (there is no god except Allah) and I shall bear witness to it in the court of Allah." Then Abu Jahl and Abdullah bin Abi Ummayah said, "O Abu Talib! Will you turn away from the religion of your father 'Abdul Muttalib?" Abu Talib replied, "I am on the religion of 'Abdul Muttalib" and passed away.

It is reported in *Sahih Muslim*[13] that 'Abbas bin 'Abdul Muttalib asked the Prophet (saw), "Abu Talib loved you profusely; he used to help and protect you despite the enmity and wrath of others. Will it benefit him?" The Messenger of Allah said, "I found him in the flames of Fire and I pulled him to its most shallow part."

It is also reported in *Sahih Muslim* that 'Aisha (ra[14]) said, "O Messenger of Allah! Ibn Jud'an established ties of kinship and fed the poor. Would that

---

[12] لاإله إلا الله

[13] *Sahih Muslim* is a collection of the sayings of Prophet Muhammad (saw).

[14] ra – *radi Allaho anh* (رضى الله عنه) means "May Allah be pleased with him." It is a prayer that is used for the Companions of Prophet Muhammad. It is *radi Allaho anhaa* (رضى الله عنها) for females.

be of any avail to him?" The Messenger of Allah (saw) said, "It would be of no avail to him as he did not ever say: O my Lord! Pardon my sins on the Day of Judgment."

A more clear narration has been reported in *Sahih Muslim* on the authority of 'Aisha (ra). 'Aisha (ra) said, "When the Prophet (saw) on his way to Badr reached Harrat-ul-Wabara (a place four miles from Madinah), a man who was known for his valor and courage met him. The Companions of the Prophet (saw) were pleased to see him. The man said, "I have come so that I may join you and get a share from the booty." The Messenger of Allah (saw) said to him, "Do you believe in Allah and His Apostle?" He said, "No." The Messenger of Allah (saw) said, "Go back. I will not seek help from a *mushrik*." The Messenger of Allah went on until we reached Shajara where the man met him again. The Messenger of Allah asked him the same question and the man gave him the same answer. The Messenger of Allah said, "Go back. I will not seek help from a *mushrik*." The man returned and overtook him at Baida'. The Messenger of Allah asked him as he had asked him previously, "Do you believe in Allah and His Apostle?" The man said, "Yes." The Messenger of Allah said to him, "Then come along with us." [Muslim, Kitabul Jihad wal Siyar, 19:4472]

Shirk disparages the noble effort and struggle of prophets and rejects the teachings of the Holy Quran. It weakens *iman* and drives a person away from the mercy of Allah.

Purity of *Iman*

Correct *iman* is the most essential requirement for being a true slave of Allah. If a person's *iman* is corrupted, none of his deeds or prayers is acceptable. On the other hand, if a person possesses correct *iman*, a small number of good deeds will be sufficient for his salvation. There is no substitute for correct *iman* and there is no salvation without it. Thus one should strive hard to correct and purify *iman*; in fact, acquiring correct *iman* should be the ultimate goal of a person's life.

To a serious reader of the Holy Quran, it becomes quite clear that the *mushrikin*[15] (polytheists) at the time of Prophet Muhammad (saw) neither rejected Allah nor considered their gods to be equal to Allah. They in fact believed that their gods were the creations of Allah and did not have the same power and authority as Allah.

---

[15] *Mushrikin* (مشركين) is the plural of *mushrik* (مشرك) which means polytheist.

Then the question is: What kind of *shirk* were they practicing? Their *shirk* was that they used to seek help and protection from their (imagined) gods, praise them, take vow in their names, swear in their names, sacrifice animals in their names and consider them as their representatives in the court of Allah. There are numerous Quranic verses such as the following which point to this kind of *shirk*:

قُل لِّمَنِ ٱلْأَرْضُ وَمَن فِيهَآ إِن كُنتُمْ تَعْلَمُونَ (84) سَيَقُولُونَ لِلَّهِ قُلْ أَفَلَا تَذَكَّرُونَ (85) قُلْ مَن رَّبُّ ٱلسَّمَٰوَٰتِ ٱلسَّبْعِ وَرَبُّ ٱلْعَرْشِ ٱلْعَظِيمِ (86) سَيَقُولُونَ لِلَّهِ قُلْ أَفَلَا تَتَّقُونَ (87) قُلْ مَنۢ بِيَدِهِ مَلَكُوتُ كُلِّ شَىْءٍ وَهُوَ يُجِيرُ وَلَا يُجَارُ عَلَيْهِ إِن كُنتُمْ تَعْلَمُونَ (88) سَيَقُولُونَ لِلَّهِ قُلْ فَأَنَّىٰ تُسْحَرُونَ (89)

Say, [O Muhammad], "To whom belongs the earth and what is contained in it, if you should know?" They will say, "To Allah." Say, "Then will you not remember?" Say, "Who is the Lord of the seven heavens and the Lord of the Great Throne?" They will say, "[They belong] to Allah." Say, "Then will you not fear Him?" Say, "Who is the One in whose hand lies the kingdom of everything and who gives protection, and no protection can be given against Him, if you have knowledge?" They will say, "(Everything belongs) to Allah." Say, "Then how have you been deluded?" [Al-Muminun, 23:84-89]

Thus those who give someone the same treatment that the *mushrikin* of Makkah used to give to their gods will fall in the same category. There will be virtually no difference between them and the *mushrikin* of Makkah.

Shah Waliyullah Dehlavi (d. 1762) has written the following in his famous book *Hujjat-Allah-al-Baalighah* (Vol. 1, pages 59-60):

There are four essential elements of *Tawheed*:

1. Believing that only Allah is *Wajib-ul-Wajud*[16] (has always been in existence and will always be in existence). This is known as *Tawheedur Rabubiyah*[17].

---

[16] *Wajib-ul-Wujud* (واجب الوجود) means that Allah is eternal. He has no beginning and no end. He is self-existent. Nothing else is self-existent.

[17] توحيدالربوبية

2. Believing that Allah is the sole Creator of the skies, worlds and heavens.
3. Believing that only Allah controls the skies, the earth and whatever lies between them.
4. Believing that no one except Allah is worthy of worship. This is known as *Tawheedul Uluhiyah*[18].

The first two are so obvious that the divine scriptures did not see the need to argue about them. Even the Jews, Christians and *mushrikin* of Makkah had no hesitation in subscribing to these concepts, as is evident from the following Quranic verse:

$$وَلَئِن سَأَلْتَهُم مَّنْ خَلَقَ ٱلسَّمَٰوَٰتِ وَٱلْأَرْضَ لَيَقُولُنَّ خَلَقَهُنَّ ٱلْعَزِيزُ ٱلْعَلِيمُ$$

And if you should ask them, "Who has created the heavens and the earth?" they would surely say, "They were created by the Exalted, the Mighty, the Knowing." [Az-Zukhruf, 43:9]

But the last two are the ones which the Holy Quran has argued about and has provided an answer to related doubts and questions.

Therefore, it means that *shirk* is not only limited to openly calling someone equal or similar to Allah, but it also includes treating someone in a way that is fitting only to Allah and to Him alone. Examples include prostrating before someone, sacrificing an animal in someone's name, taking a vow in someone's name, considering someone to be omnipresent or considering someone to have some say in the functioning of the universe; these are all acts of *shirk*. Anyone indulging in such an act is a *mushrik*[19] (polytheist) even though he may claim that the person or object he is turning to is a creation of Allah and is inferior to Allah. This is true even if the object of his devotion is a prophet, angel, saint, *jinn*[20], ghost or Satan.

This is the reason why Allah has admonished Jews and Christians who went too far in venerating and idolizing their religious leaders and priests, just as the *mushrikin* of Makkah had done with their gods:

---

[18] توحيدالالوهية
[19] مشرك
[20] Jinn (جن) is a creation which Allah created out of fire.

ٱتَّخَذُوٓاْ أَحْبَارَهُمْ وَرُهْبَٰنَهُمْ أَرْبَابًا مِّن دُونِ ٱللَّهِ وَٱلْمَسِيحَ ٱبْنَ مَرْيَمَ وَمَآ أُمِرُوٓاْ إِلَّا لِيَعْبُدُوٓاْ إِلَٰهًا وَٰحِدًاۖ لَّآ إِلَٰهَ إِلَّا هُوَۚ سُبْحَٰنَهُۥ عَمَّا يُشْرِكُونَ

They have taken their rabbis and monks as gods beside Allah, and also (they have taken) Masih, the son of Maryam (as god). And they were not commanded but to worship only One God. There is no god but He. Pure is He from what they associate with Him. [At-Taubah, 9:31]

Duty of 'Ulama

Under the influence of *shirk*, people start doing for others all those deeds which are meant exclusively for Allah; for example, sacrificing animals, consecration, prostration and supplication. Ultimately their connection with Allah gets severed; the direction of their hearts changes; their connection with their imaginary gods becomes very strong; the result of the effort of prophets gets ruined; and ignorance finally overtakes the Truth.

In every age, *'ulama*[21] (scholars) and reformers have fought against such digressions and illicit practices. According to a *hadith*[22] (saying or practice of Prophet Muhammad), *'ulama* are the heirs of prophets. But their claim of inheritance will be legitimate only if the purpose of their life and effort is the same as that of prophets - establishment of *deen*[23] (divine religion) and *Tawheed*.

Thus it is the duty of *'ulama* and reformers to strive to transform human beings into true slaves of Allah in all respects (physical, mental, emotional, and spiritual, etc.) and to establish the orders of Allah in all corners of the world, as has been ordained by Allah in the Holy Quran:

وَمَآ أَرْسَلْنَا مِن قَبْلِكَ مِن رَّسُولٍ إِلَّا نُوحِىٓ إِلَيْهِ أَنَّهُۥ لَآ إِلَٰهَ إِلَّآ أَنَا۠ فَٱعْبُدُونِ

---

[21] علماء

[22] حديث

[23] دين

> We did not send before you any messenger but We revealed to him that there is no god but I, so worship Me. [Al-Anbiya, 21:25]

$$\text{هُوَ ٱلَّذِيٓ أَرْسَلَ رَسُولَهُۥ بِٱلْهُدَىٰ وَدِينِ ٱلْحَقِّ لِيُظْهِرَهُۥ عَلَى ٱلدِّينِ كُلِّهِۦ وَلَوْ كَرِهَ ٱلْمُشْرِكُونَ}$$

> It is He Who has sent His Messenger with Guidance and the religion of Truth, that he may proclaim it over all religions, even though the pagans may detest (it). [As-Saff, 61:9]

Obstacles to True *Deen*

The true *deen* (divine religion) has always faced obstacles which basically fall into three categories: human weakness, *shirk* (polytheism) and *kufr*[24] (atheism).

Human Weakness

Man is weak by nature. He fears many things and has many hopes and desires. So he wants to believe in someone who may protect him from what he is fearful of and provide him with what he needs and desires. As a result, he is willing to submit and supplicate to anyone whom he considers to be his protector and provider.

Shirk

Shirk (polytheism) occurs when man elevates an object (which may be living, dead, imaginary, human, tree, rock, animal, etc.) to the status of Allah by believing that it has the power to harm or benefit him or has the ability to influence the operation of the universe.

Shirk is a complete system and way of life. It is mutually exclusive with Islam. It is not possible for a body, heart or mind to be home to both *shirk* and Islam. *Shirk* and Islam cannot coexist in the same space because *shirk* is as demanding as Islam. Allah has alluded to these themes in the following verses of the Holy Quran:

---

[24] كفر

وَمِنَ ٱلنَّاسِ مَن يَتَّخِذُ مِن دُونِ ٱللَّهِ أَندَادًا يُحِبُّونَهُمْ كَحُبِّ ٱللَّهِ

Yet there are men who take (for worship) others besides Allah, as equal (with Allah); they love them as they should love Allah. [Al-Baqarah, 2:165]

قَالُواْ وَهُمْ فِيهَا يَخْتَصِمُونَ (96) تَٱللَّهِ إِن كُنَّا لَفِى ضَلَٰلٍ مُّبِينٍ (97) إِذْ نُسَوِّيكُم بِرَبِّ ٱلْعَٰلَمِينَ (98)

Dwellers of Hell will say to their gods, "By Allah, we were in open error when we used to equate you with the Lord of the worlds." [Ash-Sh'uara, 26:96-98]

The seed of Islam cannot be planted until every root and fiber of *shirk* has been removed. The tree of Islam does not grow in a land that has the root or seedling of any other tree; it can bear fruit and its branches can reach the sky only if its root is deep and strong, as has been described in the Holy Quran:

أَلَمْ تَرَ كَيْفَ ضَرَبَ ٱللَّهُ مَثَلاً كَلِمَةً طَيِّبَةً كَشَجَرَةٍ طَيِّبَةٍ أَصْلُهَا ثَابِتٌ وَفَرْعُهَا فِى ٱلسَّمَآءِ (24) تُؤْتِىٓ أُكُلَهَا كُلَّ حِينٍ بِإِذْنِ رَبِّهَا وَيَضْرِبُ ٱللَّهُ ٱلْأَمْثَالَ لِلنَّاسِ لَعَلَّهُمْ يَتَذَكَّرُونَ (25)

Have you not considered how Allah presents an example, [making] a good word like a good tree, whose root is firmly fixed and its branches [high] in the sky? It produces its fruit all the time, by permission of its Lord. [Ibrahim, 14:24-25]

The tree of Islam cannot grow in the shadow of some other tree. Wherever it will be, it will be by itself. It requires an unrestricted surrounding to blossom and flourish, as Allah says in the Holy Quran:

أَلَا لِلَّهِ ٱلدِّينُ ٱلْخَالِصُ

Remember, Allah alone deserves the exclusive submission. [Az-Zumar, 39:3]

Thus those who are familiar with Allah's religion and its nature fully clear and prepare the land before they plant its seed. They weed out every fiber of ignorance, *kufr* and *shirk* from the land and turn the soil upside down, no matter how much time and effort they need to accomplish it. They may toil for their entire life, like Prophet Nooh[25] (*alaihis salaam*) who could not get more than a handful of converts, or like some other prophets who could win only a single soul on their side after their life-long struggle. Yet they strove with utmost patience and never rushed for immediate success.

Kufr

Kufr (atheism) means rejection or denial of Allah and His orders. It is in fact a revolt against Allah and is manifested in many different shapes and forms.

This term also applies to those who after becoming aware of an order of Allah and His Prophet (saw) either verbally oppose it or deliberately ignore it (without openly denouncing it). They are like the Jews, whom Allah has mentioned in the following verse:

أَفَتُؤْمِنُونَ بِبَعْضِ ٱلْكِتَـٰبِ وَتَكْفُرُونَ بِبَعْضٍ ۚ فَمَا جَزَآءُ مَن يَفْعَلُ ذَٰلِكَ مِنكُمْ إِلَّا خِزْىٌ فِى ٱلْحَيَوٰةِ ٱلدُّنْيَا ۖ وَيَوْمَ ٱلْقِيَـٰمَةِ يُرَدُّونَ إِلَىٰٓ أَشَدِّ ٱلْعَذَابِ ۗ وَمَا ٱللَّهُ بِغَـٰفِلٍ عَمَّا تَعْمَلُونَ

> So do you believe in one part of the Scripture and disbelieve in other part? Then what is the recompense for those, who do that among you, except disgrace in the worldly life; and on the Day of Resurrection, they will be sent back to the severest of punishment; and Allah is not unaware of what you do. [Al-Baqarah, 2:85]

Accepting Allah as the only God implies that the existence of all other gods must be rejected. But there are those who are not willing to do so. They are like those who despite turning their face to the (new) Qibla[26] were unwilling to turn their back on other qiblas; this refers to the order when Muslims were commanded by Allah to change their qibla from Jerusalem to Makkah in the second Hijri year.

For such people, it is hard to stay away from those practices and rituals which conflict with the orders of Allah. They jump from one system to

---

[25] Known as Noah in Western literature
[26] Qibla is the direction which Muslims face while praying

another, either for convenience or out of compulsion. The real reason for their vacillation is that they have not yet fully entered Islam. True belief in Allah demands rejection of all forms of *taghut*[27] (objects which people consider worth worshipping), as has been mentioned in the Holy Quran:

فَمَن يَكْفُرْ بِالطَّـٰغُوتِ وَيُؤْمِنْ بِاللَّهِ فَقَدِ اسْتَمْسَكَ بِالْعُرْوَةِ الْوُثْقَىٰ

So whoever disbelieves in *taghut* and believes in Allah has grasped the most trustworthy handhold. [Al-Baqarah, 2:256]

That is why the Holy Quran did not accept the claim of *iman* (faith) from those who turned for counseling or arbitration to the system or people who were opposed to Allah, as the Holy Quran states:

أَلَمْ تَرَ إِلَى الَّذِينَ يَزْعُمُونَ أَنَّهُمْ ءَامَنُوا بِمَا أُنزِلَ إِلَيْكَ وَمَا أُنزِلَ مِن قَبْلِكَ يُرِيدُونَ أَن يَتَحَاكَمُوا إِلَى الطَّـٰغُوتِ وَقَدْ أُمِرُوا أَن يَكْفُرُوا بِهِ وَيُرِيدُ الشَّيْطَـٰنُ أَن يُضِلَّهُمْ ضَلَـٰلًا بَعِيدًا

Have you not seen those who claim to have believed in what was revealed to you, [O Muhammad], and what was revealed before you? They wish to refer legislation to *taghut*, while they were commanded to reject it; and Satan wishes to lead them far astray. [An-Nisa, 4:60]

There were people who, after entering into the fold of Islam, could not fully disassociate themselves from the beliefs and rituals which they used to practice in the days of ignorance. Also, they could not rid themselves of the hatred and distaste which they used to harbor (before entering Islam) for the traditions which were commendable in Islam or were practiced by the Prophet (saw). Furthermore, they were unable to dispel the love and reverence for the practices of ignorance which were abhorred in the *Shari'ah*[28] (code of conduct) of Allah.

Proof of Faithfulness to Islam

---

[27] طاغوت

[28] شريعة

Islam also demands that all kinds of biases and prejudices (such as tribal, racial, regional, and linguistic) must be discarded as is stipulated in the core principle: Help your brother, whether he is an oppressor or an oppressed[29].

Those who, after coming into the fold of Islam, continue to observe rules and regulations of the days of ignorance to determine what is good and what is bad, and what is important and what is not are still on shaky ground.

The proof of one's faithfulness to Islam is that *kufr* - its ways, rituals and values - should become totally repugnant to him; even the thought of going back to them becomes intolerable to him. It is one of the signs of a *momin*[30] (believer) that he prefers death to even the slightest indulgence in *kufr*, as has been mentioned in the following *hadith* of *Sahih Bukhari*[31]:

> Narrated Anas: The Prophet (saw) said, "Whoever possesses the following three qualities will taste the sweetness of *iman*: 1) Allah and His Messenger become dearer to him than everything else; 2) He loves a person only for Allah's sake; 3) He hates going back to *kufr* as much as he hates being thrown into fire." [*Sahih Bukhari, Kitabul Iman*]

This was the condition of the Companions of the Prophet (saw). They had developed utmost distaste for their past lives, its customs, traditions and manners. There was nothing more reprehensible to them than *kufr* and *shirk*. They felt ashamed and remorseful in recounting their past. Allah has mentioned it in the following verse of the Holy Quran:

$$ \text{لَـٰكِنَّ ٱللَّهَ حَبَّبَ إِلَيْكُمُ ٱلْإِيمَـٰنَ وَزَيَّنَهُۥ فِى قُلُوبِكُمْ وَكَرَّهَ إِلَيْكُمُ ٱلْكُفْرَ وَٱلْفُسُوقَ وَٱلْعِصْيَانَ} $$

---

29 Anas ibn Malik reported: The Messenger of Allah said, "Help your brother, whether he is an   oppressor or an oppressed." It was asked, "O Prophet of Allah, we help the one being   oppressed but how do we help an oppressor?" He said, "By preventing him from oppressing others." [*Sahih Bukhari, Kitabul Mazalim wal Ghazab*]

30 مومن

31 *Sahih Bukhari* is a collection of the sayings of Prophet Muhammad (saw).

Allah has endeared *iman* to you and has beautified it in your hearts, and has made *kufr*, wickedness and disobedience (to Allah and His Messenger) hateful to you. [Al-Hujurat, 49:7]

One of the signs of ignorance is that when an order of Allah or His Prophet (saw) is presented, it is rebutted by a tradition of the past or a practice of the forefathers, as has been mentioned by the Holy Quran:

وَإِذَا قِيلَ لَهُمُ ٱتَّبِعُوا۟ مَآ أَنزَلَ ٱللَّهُ قَالُوا۟ بَلْ نَتَّبِعُ مَآ أَلْفَيْنَا عَلَيْهِ ءَابَآءَنَآ أَوَلَوْ كَانَ ءَابَآؤُهُمْ لَا يَعْقِلُونَ شَيْـًٔا وَلَا يَهْتَدُونَ

And when it is said to them, "Follow what Allah has revealed," they say, "Rather, we will follow that which we found our fathers doing." Even though their fathers understood nothing, nor were they guided? [Al-Baqarah, 2:170]

بَلْ قَالُوٓا۟ إِنَّا وَجَدْنَآ ءَابَآءَنَا عَلَىٰٓ أُمَّةٍ وَإِنَّا عَلَىٰٓ ءَاثَٰرِهِم مُّهْتَدُونَ

Rather, they say, "Indeed, we found our fathers upon a religion, and we are in their footsteps [rightly] guided." [Az-Zukhraf, 43:22]

قَالُوا۟ يَٰشُعَيْبُ أَصَلَوٰتُكَ تَأْمُرُكَ أَن نَّتْرُكَ مَا يَعْبُدُ ءَابَآؤُنَآ أَوْ أَن نَّفْعَلَ فِىٓ أَمْوَٰلِنَا مَا نَشَٰٓؤُا۟

They said, "O Shu'aib! Does your prayer command you that we should leave what our fathers worship or not do with our wealth as we please? [Hud, 11:87]

If one has not fully dissociated himself from all other gods and has not completely surrendered to Allah, it means that he has not yet fully migrated to Islam from ignorance. One must submit and surrender to Allah as Prophet Ibrahim (*alaihis salaam*) did when he was commanded to do so, as is mentioned in the Holy Quran:

إِذْ قَالَ لَهُۥ رَبُّهُۥٓ أَسْلِمْ قَالَ أَسْلَمْتُ لِرَبِّ ٱلْعَٰلَمِينَ

When his Lord said to him, "Submit", he said "I have submitted to the Lord of the worlds." [Al-Baqarah, 2:131]

Every Muslim is commanded to do the same:

$$\text{فَإِلَـٰهُكُمْ إِلَـٰهٌ وَاحِدٌ فَلَهُ أَسْلِمُو}$$

> So, your God is One God. Therefore, to Him alone you must submit. [Al-Hajj, 22:34]

If it is not so, it is a revolt against Allah. That is why Allah has used the word *silm*[32] (full submission) for complete Islam, as is mentioned in the following verse of the Holy Quran:

$$\text{يَـٰأَيُّهَا الَّذِينَ ءَامَنُوا ادْخُلُوا فِي السِّلْمِ كَآفَّةً وَلَا تَتَّبِعُوا خُطُوَاتِ الشَّيْطَـٰنِ إِنَّهُ لَكُمْ عَدُوٌّ مُّبِينٌ}$$

> O you who believe, enter into Islam completely [and perfectly] and do not follow the footsteps of Satan. Indeed, he is to you an open enemy. [Al-Baqarah, 2:208]

It should be kept in mind that ignorance (in scope and definition) does not refer only to the life of Arabs before the coming of Prophet Muhammad (saw). It also includes every system and lifestyle that is devoid of divine revelations, the Books of Allah and the teachings of prophets. It may include Mozdakism (a reformed version of Zoroastrianism) of Iran, Brahmanism of India, Paganism of Egypt, Suryani of Turkey, Western civilization or un-Islamic practices of a Muslim society. It does not matter if it is ancient or modern.

Fighting *Kufr* and *Shirk*

We need to rely on the understanding and guidance of prophets in fighting *kufr* and *shirk*. It is not possible to defend Islam without understanding and recognizing the boundaries that they have drawn between Islam, *kufr* and *shirk*. A slight misstep or negligence in this matter may disfigure and distort Islam in the same way as Judaism, Christianity and Hinduism.

'Ulama (scholars) who are the true heirs of prophets also ought to possess the same vision and foresight as that of prophets. They should be able to immediately recognize *kufr* and its manifestations regardless of which cloak it dons or which shape it acquires. They should not falter in

---

[32] سلم

identifying it. They should not hesitate in fighting and eradicating it. They should not compromise with it at any cost.

They may be ridiculed, mocked or given derogatory names by the so-called liberal and secular-minded people (who consider it an act of injustice to differentiate between places of worship, be it for idol worship or Allah). Despite all odds, they must continue their struggle with full devotion and determination. It is in fact due to the efforts and sacrifices of such *'ulama* that Islam is still intact in its purest form and has not met the fate of the religions of Jews, Christians and Hindus.

Prophet Muhammad's Conscience

Prophet Muhammad (saw) was the most enlightened person about *Tawheed*. He was the greatest inviter towards it. He had the most love for Allah. He sacrificed most for Allah.

The Prophet's conscience for the greatness of Allah was such that when a person said, "One who obeys Allah and His Prophet will be guided and one who disobeys them will go astray," he could not tolerate it and said to that person, "You do not know how to speak. You should have said: One who disobeys Allah and His Prophet will go astray." The Prophet (saw) did not like his name to be mentioned in a way that might give even the slightest impression of it being on the same level as the name of Allah.

Similarly, when a person said, "If you and Allah desire, this thing will happen," the Prophet (saw) immediately said, "Did you make me equal to Allah? No. It is only the will of Allah which makes things happen." This was the state of the Prophet's conscience.

A Few Illustrations of *Tawheed*

Sheikh Abdur Qadir Jeelani (d. 1166), who is regarded as a great scholar and spiritual figure by people of all affiliations and regions, has explained *Tawheed* by an excellent analogy in which he has also shown the fallacy of going to sources other than Allah for the purpose of alleviating a problem or receiving a benefit:

> Consider the entire creation as a man whose hands have
> been tied by a powerful king who rules a vast kingdom.
> The king has tied that person's legs, put a noose around

his neck and hanged him from a pine tree which is located on the bank of a river which is very deep, wide and violent. The king has seated himself on a huge chair which is very high and magnificent and is beyond the reach of anyone. He has also accumulated by his side a huge pile of arrows, spears, swords and other weapons.

Given this situation, who should one fear or look for help - the king or the person who is hanging from the tree? If one chooses to approach the person hanging from the tree, he will be deemed insane and will not deserve to be called even an animal.

Sheikh Sharfuddin Yahya Maneri (d. 1291), while describing the greatness and magnanimity of Allah, wrote a letter which makes a person shiver and tremble with awe and fear:

Allah does what He wills. He is not affected by anyone's demise or emancipation. Consider (the helplessness of) a person who is dying of thirst although rivers are flowing under his feet, but is not able to get a drop of water from it. An oracle from a distance says to him, "I bring thousands of faithful and honest people to dark jungles and arid deserts and kill them so that their eyes and cheeks are devoured by crows and vultures. And if someone objects to it, I put a seal on his tongue and tell him, "Both the victims and the birds belong to me. So who are you to question what I do."

D'awah of Tawheed in India

India is the home of a number of major polytheistic religions and the foundation of Islam has always been weak there due to some historical reasons. There was a time (16th century AD) when Islam became so garbled and misrepresented in India that it appeared that the light of Islam would become obscure and unidentifiable forever in that part of the world.

At that very time, Mujaddid Alf Thani (d. 1624) started his reformist movement which was modeled on the work of prophets. He refused to prostrate before the Moghul Emperor Jehangir (1605-27). In his writings, he articulated the oneness of Allah and argued that Allah is the only one who deserves to be worshipped and be the object of prostration. He condemned the customs and practices of ignorance, polytheism and paganism and strictly instructed his followers to discard such practices.

In one of his letters[33], Mujaddid Alf Thani wrote: "My dear friend! After traveling the path of *suluk*[34] (spiritual mentoring) and vanquishing all my feelings, emotions and desires, I have realized that the sole objective of all these exercises is to attain *ikhlas*[35] (sincerity) which demands rejection of all deities, internal as well as external."

In another letter he wrote: "The real cause of all the internal (spiritual) ailments is the attachment and occupation with objects other than Allah. Unless complete freedom is achieved from these objects, it is not possible to attain salvation because there is no room for any partnership in the court of Allah. Obedience and worship is only for Allah. Thus it is a matter of great shame and ignominy to love someone more intensely than Allah."

The sole objective of *tariqat*[36] (spiritual mentoring) and *tasawwuf*[37] (mysticism) is to develop a relationship with Allah so that there remains no veil or medium between Allah and His slave and there is never a vacillation or wavering in this relationship. But this cannot be achieved until one becomes fully convinced that no creation in the universe has any power or ability to cause any harm or benefit to anyone [except with the permission of Allah] and the heart and mind become completely free from the love and greatness of every created being. In other words, both fear and hope must be associated with Allah alone. This is what *ikhlas* is all about and this is what the prophets strove to inculcate in people.

Mir Syed 'Ali Hamdani

Mir Syed 'Ali Hamdani (d. 1384) was a great reformer who is credited with the spread of Islam in Kashmir. He was originally from Khatlon, a province in the Central Asian country of Tajikistan.

The question is: What brought Mir Hamdani to Kashmir from Khatlon? Was it the beauty and splendor of the valley of Kashmir or the high peaks

---

[33] Originally in Persian

[34] سلوك

[35] اخلاص

[36] طريقت

[37] تصوف

of Mount Everest? Khalton itself was very beautiful. Then, why did he come to Kashmir?

Let me tell you what brought Mir Hamdani to Kashmir. It was his conscience and sense of responsibility. He was a lover of Allah. He was an intimate knower of Allah. He was a lover of Prophet Muhammad (saw). His sense of responsibility for Islam was extraordinarily high. Thus when he heard that Kashmir was a vast valley, the people living there were ignorant of Allah and worshipping many objects – anything that appeared to have some power, some ability to harm or benefit, some beauty or some unusual capacity – he set out for that land with the message of *Tawheed*.

In my opinion, had he not taken that task on himself, the valley of Kashmir would have remained ignorant of Allah and His Prophet (saw). On the east of the valley, nearby India on the foothills of the Himalayas was full of *'ulama*, *madaaris* (Islamic schools of learning) and *khanqah* (seats of spiritual mentoring); on the west, there were numerous spiritual hubs present in between Khalton and the valley; but the valley had not seen the light of Islam yet.

Those who are determined in their mission do not debate whether it is their personal duty or not. They consider it to be their personal obligation and they set out to do what needs to be done. Countless hurdles and thousands of obstacles fail to dampen their zeal and resolve. They treat it as a call from the heavens. They do not care about the consequences. This is what brought Mir Hamdani to Kashmir.

Mir Hamdani clearly felt that he was answerable to Allah. He envisioned that it was the Day of Judgment, Allah was seated on His majestic throne, all of His prophets and friends were standing under the shade of His throne and a question was asked, "Mir Hamdani! You knew that there was a piece of land on the earth where people were worshipping idols and seeking their help. How did you tolerate it?"

This was the sight in front of Mir Hamdani. If all the *'ulama* and wise people of the world would have wanted to convince him that the above question was not directed to him, he would have replied, "No. That question is directed to me. My conscience does not allow me to sit at rest while people in even a small part of this vast world are worshipping idols, fearing them, begging them for their needs, and believing that these idols are controlling their destiny, providing sustenance and giving children. If I know that there is one such individual in the North or South Pole or on top of Mount Everest, it becomes my duty to reach him and convey to him the message of Allah."

Mir Hamdani understood the meaning of the following verses of the Holy Quran:

$$أَلَا لَهُ ٱلْخَلْقُ وَٱلْأَمْرُ$$

Lo! To Him alone belong the creation and the command. [Al-A'raf, 7:54]

$$وَسِعَ كُرْسِيُّهُ ٱلسَّمَٰوَٰتِ وَٱلْأَرْضَ$$

His throne includes the heavens and the earth. [Al-Baqarah, 2:255]

Allah did not hand over the administration of the universe to someone after creating it. He is the Creator as well as the Sustainer, the Controller and the Administrator. The universe is not like the Taj Mahal which was built by Emperor Shah Jehan with the help of architects and laborers from Turkestan and then its ownership and administration continued to change hands.

Prophet Yaqoob's Example

We can see an excellent example of a great conscience in Prophet Yaqoob[38] (*alaihis salaam*). When he was about to depart from this world, he collected all of his children and grandchildren and said to them, "My dear children! I will not lie down with peace in my grave until you assure me as to whom you will worship after me." Upon that they resolutely said, "Do not be worried. We will only worship your Lord and the Lord of your fathers and forefathers Ibrahim, Ismail[39] and Ishaq[40]", as has been mentioned in the Holy Quran:

$$قَالُوا۟ نَعْبُدُ إِلَٰهَكَ وَإِلَٰهَ ءَابَآئِكَ إِبْرَٰهِۦمَ وَإِسْمَٰعِيلَ وَإِسْحَٰقَ إِلَٰهًا$$
$$وَٰحِدًا وَنَحْنُ لَهُۥ مُسْلِمُونَ$$

---

[38] Known as Jacob in Western literature
[39] Known as Ishmael in Western literature
[40] Known as Isaac in Western literature

They said, "We will worship your God and the God of your fathers, Ibrahim and Ismail and Ishaq - one God. And we are Muslims [in submission] to Him." [Al-Baqarah, 2:133]

They said to Prophet Yaqoob, "Why are you asking this question? What is your concern? Be assured that we will not forsake the belief of *Tawheed* which you have planted and nurtured in our hearts since our childhood. We will not abandon the worship of the One God whom Ibrahim, Ismail and Ishaq used to worship." This reassured Prophet Yaqoob (*alaihis salaam*) and he departed from this world in a state of joy and happiness. Prophet Yaqoob (*alaihis salaam*) was worried that his progeny may meet the same fate as those who went astray after their forefathers left the world.

This was the message which every prophet brought and all the reformers, revivalists and *waliyallah*[41] carried across the world.

Shirk and Falsehood are Twins

Allah says in the Holy Quran:

إِنَّ ٱلَّذِينَ ٱتَّخَذُواْ ٱلْعِجْلَ سَيَنَالُهُمْ غَضَبٌ مِّن رَّبِّهِمْ وَذِلَّةٌ فِى ٱلْحَيَوٰةِ ٱلدُّنْيَا وَكَذَالِكَ نَجْزِى ٱلْمُفْتَرِينَ

Surely, those who have taken the calf (as god) shall be seized by Allah's wrath and by humiliation in the worldly life. That is how we recompense the fabricators. [Al-A'raf, 7:152]

The punishment that is meted out to those who indulge in fabricating falsehood also applies to those who indulge in *shirk* because *shirk* is always based upon fabricated stories. Falsehood and *shirk* are like twins as Allah has said:

فَٱجْتَنِبُواْ ٱلرِّجْسَ مِنَ ٱلْأَوْثَانِ وَٱجْتَنِبُواْ قَوْلَ ٱلزُّورِ

So refrain from the filth of the idols and refrain from a word of falsehood. [Al-Hajj, 22:30]

---

[41] ولي الله - friends/lovers of Allah

وَمَن يُشْرِكْ بِٱللَّهِ فَقَدِ ٱفْتَرَىٰٓ إِثْمًا عَظِيمًا

Whoever ascribes a partner to Allah fabricates a terrible falsehood. [An-Nisa, 4:48]

Tawheed – Universal Distinction of Muslims

Tawheed is the unique identity and symbol of Muslims all over the world. It encompasses all aspects of their life, be it religious, social, or cultural. From the minarets of their *masaajid*[42] (places of worship), a call is made five times a day that there is no one worthy of worship except Allah. Their houses as well as the places of social and community gatherings must also be free from the influence of idol worshipping and *shirk*; pictures (of humans and animals), statues and idols are prohibited, even in the shape of children's toys.

It is prohibited for Muslims to bow down or stand with folded hands in front of pictures or statues or to pay homage by placing wreaths or garland of flowers – a common practice in some parts of the world during the celebration of national days, birthdays of national heroes and flag hoisting.

Tawheed –Source of Strength

One who is aware of *Tawheed* relies only on Allah, resorts to Him in need, offers thanks to Him in ease and comfort, remains faithful to Him and worships Him only.

Tawheed is the greatest source of strength, as Allah mentions in the Holy Quran:

سَنُلْقِى فِى قُلُوبِ ٱلَّذِينَ كَفَرُوا۟ ٱلرُّعْبَ بِمَآ أَشْرَكُوا۟ بِٱللَّهِ مَا لَمْ يُنَزِّلْ بِهِۦ سُلْطَٰنًا ۖ وَمَأْوَىٰهُمُ ٱلنَّارُ ۚ وَبِئْسَ مَثْوَى ٱلظَّٰلِمِينَ

We shall put awe into the hearts of those who disbelieve, since they have associated with Allah something for which He has not sent any authority. Their ultimate place is the Fire; and evil is the abode of the unjust. [Al-Imran, 3:151]

---

[42] مساجد – it is the plural of مسجد

Allah has put certain properties in things; for example, poison has a property (of killing), medicine has a property (of curing), water has a property (of quenching thirst), and fire has a property (of burning). Similarly, *shirk* has a property and it is the property of weakness. Likewise, *Tawheed* has a property and it is the property of strength, boldness and fearlessness.

Thus the most important need of a person is to correct his *'aqeedah* and develop a strong relationship with Allah in accordance with the teachings of Prophet Ibrahim (*alaihis salaam*), Prophet Muhammad (saw), and the Holy Quran. This relationship with Allah needs to be constantly strengthened and fortified because Satan is always looking for ways to undermine and corrupt it; a thief attacks only those who possess wealth and does not bother those who possess nothing.

When a person acquires correct understanding of *Tawheed*, he understands that the entire universe is functioning under a well-managed and well-controlled system and every object of the universe is running in a well-coordinated way. He can fully understand the intricacies and nuances of life. He can build a society on righteousness, piety, justice, tolerance and mutual co-operation. He can overcome all kinds of prejudices. He can view the entire mankind as a single family. He can combine *deen* (divine religion) and *dunya*[43] (worldly pursuit) and fulfill the needs of both this life and the Hereafter.

Pure *Tawheed*

There is only one Creator of this universe. He has been in existence forever and He will be in existence forever. He is praiseworthy and each of His qualities is perfect. He is free from all defects and blemishes. He is all-knowing. The entire universe is subservient to His will. He is alert. He sees all. He hears all. There is no one like Him. He does not need anyone's help. There is no one who shares any responsibility with Him in running this universe. He is the only one worthy of worship. He is the only one who cures the sick. He is the only one who alleviates difficulties and hardships. He is the only one who provides sustenance to everyone.

Treating others (other than Allah) as god, kneeling down or prostrating in front of them, beseeching them for help, expecting them to do something which is beyond the capacity of human beings such as to know what is

______

[43] دنیا

hidden in the heart of a person, to change the fate or destiny of a person, to bless someone with a child, etc. - these are acts of *shirk* which is the greatest sin and cannot be forgiven without penitence. It is only Allah who is capable of making these things happen, as the Holy Quran says:

إِنَّمَآ أَمۡرُهُۥ إِذَآ أَرَادَ شَيۡئًا أَن يَقُولَ لَهُۥ كُن فَيَكُونُ

Verily, when He intends a thing, His Command is "Be" and it is! [Ya-Sin, 36:82]

Allah does not incarnate Himself in any shape or form. He is not limited to any direction. What He wills happens. What He does not will does not happen. He is absolutely independent. He needs nothing from anyone, nor does anyone possess any control or influence over Him. No one can question Him about what He does and there is no one above Him. Wisdom is His attribute. His every act is full of wisdom and goodness. Whatever good or bad comes, it comes because that is His will and there is wisdom in it. He knows things before they come into existence and He is the cause of existence of everything.

Chapter 2 - Prophethood

There are several questions which intuitively arise in a human mind. They continuously unsettle him and he feels compelled to search for their answer. The questions are: Who is running this universe? What are His attributes? How is He related to us? How are we related to Him? What are His likes and dislikes? What is the ultimate goal of our life? What is the end-point of this universe?

These questions are very logical and a person is duly entitled to ask about them. It is his right to ask who created the world in which he lives and who is running it. Furthermore, he cannot develop a close relationship with his Creator unless he knows Him well. It is true in our everyday life also that we cannot develop a hearty and robust relationship with a person unless we know him intimately and understand his temperament, likes and dislikes.

If we know nothing about our Creator except that He exists - we are unaware of His power, authority, knowledge, mercy, compassion, beauty and magnificence and do not know how much we depend on Him for our needs, survival and existence - we cannot develop the kind of relationship that we ought to have with Him.

Equally valid and logical is the following question: What does He as the owner of this universe demand from us as we live in His kingdom? It in fact becomes our duty to find out what the rules and regulations of His kingdom are.

It is also important to know the purpose of this life and what is going to happen after this life. This knowledge is pertinent not only to the future but also to the present. If a person knows that there will be another life after death, he will be held accountable for what he does in this life and will be rewarded and punished for his deeds, his lifestyle will be very different from that of a person who has no concept of any life after this life. That is why this question is extremely crucial and any delay in finding its answer is fraught with great danger; a proper plan cannot be chalked out for this life without it.

These are the basic questions. Our success and salvation depend on them. A slight mistake or negligence in finding their answer may doom us forever. We have only one life and only one chance. It is too precious to be blown away in mere speculation, guesswork and experimentation.

In addition to the above questions, there are many more which are related to our everyday life and need to be answered correctly: How are we related to our surrounding and how is it related to us? Where do we stand in the larger picture of this universe? Are we subordinate to someone or are we fully independent? Do we have any responsibility? If yes, what is the scope of our responsibility? Are we answerable to someone for our deeds? Are we the outright owner or mere custodian of our abilities and faculties? How are we supposed to utilize the resources that we possess?

Getting Answers to Our Questions

There can be only two ways to get answers to these questions. Either we rely solely on our own intellect, know-how, experiences and observations, or we approach some other sources or group of individuals.

Approach# 1

If we rely solely on our own knowledge, the most that we can conclude is that there is a creator of this universe. But the question still remains: What are His attributes and qualities? The answer to this question is beyond our comprehension because there is no similarity between the Creator and the created. Since all of our observations and experiences are based on our interactions with created beings, we cannot correctly imagine the Creator on our own.

Then the next difficult question is: What does He want from us and what are His likes and dislikes? It is our everyday experience that it is very difficult to discover, even in the case of our closest friends and relatives, what exactly they like and dislike. We sometimes fail miserably in this regard. So how difficult will it be to correctly discern the likes and dislikes of someone whom we do not know and cannot visualize?

The other problem with this approach (of relying solely upon our own knowledge and experience) is that different people reach different conclusions about this matter. One person concludes that this universe came into existence on its own, is running on its own and will perish one day on its own. Another person concludes that this universe was created by someone who thereafter disassociated himself from it and handed over the responsibility of running it to others. There are others who deify everything that appears to have some ability to harm or benefit.

There are yet others who believe that the human being is an advanced form of animal; he has his own needs and desires; he has unlimited power and potential; he is not answerable to anyone; there is nothing beyond his reach; there is nothing in the universe that he cannot explore, discover and control; only might and power matter in this life; and the concepts of morality, righteousness, sin and vice are meaningless.

There are philosophers and thinkers who, after accepting the existence of god, labored hard to speculate and identify the attributes of their imagined god. It is strange that some of the attributes that they associated with their gods were too derogatory and reprehensible to be associated with even the human beings.

There are many more questions that need to be addressed. What is the status of man in this universe? What is the purpose of his life? How should he deal with other human beings and creations? Is he answerable to someone? How much free will and independence does he have? All of these questions in fact stem from the main question: Who is the Creator of this universe? If the main question gets answered correctly, all others will get answered automatically. On the other hand, if one stumbles in finding the correct answer to the main question, he is bound to get lost with respect to other questions as well.

Approach# 2

If we approach other sources to get answers to our questions, we must ask the following: Upon which other sources can we rely? If it is a group of learned and wise people, the next question arises: In what respect are they more qualified and competent than us and what knowledge do they have about the metaphysical world? The learned and wise people themselves concede that these questions pertain to what is beyond the reach of the human sensory systems (of touching, hearing, seeing, smelling and tasting) and human cognition. So how can they lead us in this endeavor and how can we rely upon their judgment? The Holy Quran has rightly said about them:

هَٰأَنتُمْ هَٰؤُلَاءِ حَاجَجْتُمْ فِيمَا لَكُم بِهِ عِلْمٌ فَلِمَ تُحَاجُّونَ فِيمَا لَيْسَ لَكُم بِهِ عِلْمٌ ۚ وَاللَّهُ يَعْلَمُ وَأَنتُمْ لَا تَعْلَمُونَ

> You have argued about that of which you have some
> knowledge, but why do you argue about that of which you
> have no knowledge? Allah knows, while you know not.
> [Al-Imran, 3:66]

Then the only choice that is left for us is to approach those whose knowledge concerning these questions is deep and reliable; who have acquired that knowledge through definite means; who have witnessed and experienced them in the same way as ordinary human beings witness and experience things of this life through their sensory systems; and are endowed with an additional sense which enables them to see and know what is beyond the reach of ordinary human beings.

Such people are none but the prophets. Their impeccable character, lifestyle, honesty, wisdom and justice testify that they belong to a very different category and have access to the knowledge and enlightenment that is inaccessible to ordinary human beings. The miracles that took place at their hands further testify that they are indeed prophets and they are recipients of *wahi*[1] (divine revelation).

Philosophers and thinkers cannot claim the veracity of their knowledge and theories (about the universe, its creator, Life Hereafter, etc.) with full certainty. They cannot provide any concrete evidence to support their theories. Their conjectures are basically derived from a set of principles which they have themselves formulated according to their own understanding, thinking and experience.

On the other hand, prophets claim the veracity of their knowledge with full conviction. Not only do they proclaim the existence of Allah and His attributes, but they also claim that they listen to Him, they talk to Him, they receive revelation from Him and His angels come to them. They are so convinced about Allah, His attributes, their own prophethood and their message that they do not waver in their conviction even for a moment under any condition.

Prophets have such a vantage point that they can see the *ghaib* (unseen, to the extent that Allah wills) and have the full spectrum of the Hereafter in front of their eyes. To those who argue with prophets without seeing what prophets can see, prophets can say, "Our eyes see what you cannot see. Our ears hear what you cannot hear. Your salvation lies only in believing

---

[1] وحی

in what we are telling you after seeing what we have seen and after hearing what we have heard."[2]

As the Holy Quran mentions, when people argued with Prophet Ibrahim (*alaihis salaam*) about Allah and His attributes, he simply said to them:

وَحَآجَّهُۥ قَوْمُهُۥ قَالَ أَتُحَـٰجُّوٓنِّى فِى ٱللَّهِ وَقَدْ هَدَٰنِ

Do you argue with me concerning Allah while He has guided me? [Al-An'am, 6:80]

Prophet Hud (*alaihis salaam*) said the same to his people:

قَالَ يَـٰقَوْمِ أَرَءَيْتُمْ إِن كُنتُ عَلَىٰ بَيِّنَةٍ مِّن رَّبِّى وَءَاتَىٰنِى رَحْمَةً مِّنْ عِندِهِۦ فَعُمِّيَتْ عَلَيْكُمْ أَنُلْزِمُكُمُوهَا وَأَنتُمْ لَهَا كَـٰرِهُونَ

He said: "O my people! Tell me, if I have a clear proof from my Lord, and a mercy (Prophethood) has come to me from Him, but that (mercy) has been obscured from your sight. Shall we compel you to accept it when you have a strong hatred for it? [Hud, 11:28]

Allah says about Prophet Muhammad (saw):

وَمَا يَنطِقُ عَنِ ٱلْهَوَىٰٓ (3) إِنْ هُوَ إِلَّا وَحْىٌ يُوحَىٰ (4)

Nor does he speak from [his own] inclination. It is not but a revelation revealed to him. [An-Najm, 53:3-4]

Allah further says in the Holy Quran about Prophet Muhammad (saw):

____

[2] In his sermon at the mountain of Safa, Prophet Muhammad (saw) beautifully described the difference between a prophet and an ordinary person. He stood at the top of the mountain and asked his people, "How have you found my conduct so far?" All said, "We have always found you honest and trustworthy." The Prophet then asked, "If I say to you that an enemy is behind this mountain and he is about to attack you, will you believe in it?" They said, "There is no reason for us not to believe in it." The Prophet then said, "I warn you that the punishment of Allah is about to come." In this sermon, the Prophet mentioned only two qualities: 1) Honesty and trustworthiness, and 2) Prophetic knowledge of the unseen which ordinary human beings do not possess.

مَا زَاغَ ٱلْبَصَرُ وَمَا طَغَىٰ (17) لَقَدْ رَأَىٰ مِنْ ءَايَٰتِ رَبِّهِ ٱلْكُبْرَىٰ (18)

The sight [of the Prophet] did not swerve, nor did it transgress [its limit]. He certainly saw of the greatest signs of his Lord. [An-Najm, 53:17-18]

مَا كَذَبَ ٱلْفُؤَادُ مَا رَأَىٰ (11) أَفَتُمَٰرُونَهُ عَلَىٰ مَا يَرَىٰ (12)

The heart [of the Prophet] did not lie [about] what it saw. So will you dispute with him over what he saw? [An-Najm, 53:11-12]

Allah further says in the Holy Quran about those who argue with prophets:

إِن يَتَّبِعُونَ إِلَّا ٱلظَّنَّ وَمَا تَهْوَى ٱلْأَنفُسُ وَلَقَدْ جَآءَهُم مِّن رَّبِّهِمُ ٱلْهُدَىٰ

They are following nothing but speculation and what their own souls desire, although guidance from their Lord has surely reached them. [An-Najm, 53:23]

وَمَا لَهُم بِهِ مِنْ عِلْمٍ إِن يَتَّبِعُونَ إِلَّا ٱلظَّنَّ وَإِنَّ ٱلظَّنَّ لَا يُغْنِى مِنَ ٱلْحَقِّ شَيْـًٔا

They do not have knowledge about it. They follow nothing but speculation and speculation is of no avail in (the matter of) Truth. [An-Najm, 53:28]

Life cannot be Fully Explained without Prophets

Without receiving an answer to the above mentioned metaphysical questions, we cannot behave better than animals. Without the guidance of prophets and divine revelations, we cannot gain a full understanding of our own life, know who is controlling and sustaining the universe or understand how the universe is functioning. If we rely solely on our own intellect and understanding, this life will appear haphazard, chaotic and disorganized like the scattered pages of a book whose theme is not clear and whose author is inconclusive about the message he wants to convey.

The discoveries which scientists have made while exploring the universe and human life are astonishing. The way engineers have harnessed and conquered natural resources is mind-boggling. The vast amount of knowledge that humans have accumulated in arts, science and technology is remarkable.

Yet these achievements and advancements, as spectacular and intriguing as they may appear, affect only a small aspect of human life and do not answer the very basic questions - What is the purpose of life? Who is the nucleus of the universe? Who is running the universe? These questions are crucial as they determine how a person conducts his life and fulfills his responsibilities.

The main reason why these remarkable accomplishments have failed to answer these questions is that philosophers, thinkers and scientists started their journey of discovery and exploration in a very wrong direction. Instead of trying to discover the creator of the universe, they spent all of their energies and talents in probing everything else.

If we look at the universe through the lens of a prophet, it appears to be running perfectly with all of its components fully synchronized and working under a central command for a well-defined purpose. It is like a very complex machine which has many parts and each part is playing an essential role in tandem with other parts; or, it is like a huge factory with hundreds of machines which are well coordinated and are operating under the supervision of a very competent and knowledgeable operator.

Difference between Prophets and Philosophers

Let me give an example to explain how prophets are different from philosophers, thinkers, and other intellectuals with respect to their approach towards the universe.

A group of intellectuals and researchers with different interests and expertise entered a city. Some of them were geographers. They started investigating the boundaries of the city, its area, its latitude and longitude, its rivers and mountains, the sources of the rivers, and the crops that grow there.

Some were historians and archeologists. They started investigating when the city came into existence, which archeological sites are in the city and what their history is.

Some were geologists. They started investigating the mines and minerals buried underneath the city.

Some were meteorologists. They established an observatory and started investigating the stars, planets, weather, earthquakes, rain and wind.

Some were chemists. They established a chemical laboratory and began investigating herbs and chemicals and started conducting tests and experiments to observe chemical reactions.

Some were linguists. They started investigating the dialects and languages spoken by people of the city. They studied local literature and worked on developing a dictionary and the rules of grammar.

Some were interested in flowers, vegetation and the scenic beauty of the city. They composed poems to express their thoughts and feelings.

Some were sociologists. They engaged themselves in studying social habits and cultural traditions of the city.

There were some who were expert in civic administration. They developed proposals to improve the administration and facilities of the city.

All these groups started working in their respective areas of interest with full dedication and commitment.

Now a person enters the city, looks at everything with a sharp eye, listens to everything with an attentive ear, but does not engage himself in any of the above activities. Issues such as the area of the city, its history and identification of the minerals buried underneath its surface, are of no interest to him. The questions which are important to him are: Who created the city with all of its beauty and grandeur? Who is the master of the city? Who is controlling its operation? Who are the inhabitants of the city? How is the relationship between the master and the inhabitants?

He instead becomes the medium and interpreter between the master and the inhabitants of the city. He communicates the orders of the master to the inhabitants. By doing so, he has acquired a position that no group of investigators can match. Without his services, the entire city will simply become a museum and tourist attraction.

Prophets are like the person who has become a medium between the master of the city and the inhabitants of the city. Their mission and vision is quite different from that of others. They do not get distracted by the observable things of the universe. They do not occupy themselves in exploring and beautifying things which are ordinarily visible to a human eye.

Philosophers and thinkers, in comparison to prophets, are like ignorant children (who are playing with beautiful sea-shells on the seashore) in front of an experienced sailor. They know very little about this life and they know absolutely nothing about the Life Hereafter. Thus they need guidance of prophets as much as an ordinary uneducated villager needs.

Uniqueness of Prophets

Prophets are directly connected to the Creator of things (both seen and unseen). They see His clear signs in both the living and material objects of the universe. They see this universe as mere manifestation of His commands. They see His magnificence in every object of the universe. They do not find any break-down anywhere in His kingdom. They do not see any interruption in the execution of His orders. They see every mighty and powerful being in servitude to Him. They see His hand in everything that happens. They see Him holding the earth and sky. All of these phenomena become reality to them.

The greatness of Allah and His kingdom becomes unveiled to prophets. It is the highest form of knowledge and enlightenment. This knowledge is out of the reach of philosophers and thinkers. The knowledge of philosophers and thinkers is infinitesimal compared to the knowledge of prophets, as Allah has said in the Holy Quran:

وَكَذَٰلِكَ نُرِىٓ إِبْرَٰهِيمَ مَلَكُوتَ ٱلسَّمَٰوَٰتِ وَٱلْأَرْضِ وَلِيَكُونَ مِنَ ٱلْمُوقِنِينَ

> In this way We showed Ibrahim Our kingdom of the heavens and the earth so that he might have certainty of faith. [Al-An'am, 6:75]

Prophets exemplify the best character, purest heart and extraordinary wisdom. As soon as they reach the age of adolescence, they earnestly start searching for the real Creator and Master of the universe and they do not rest until they find Him. Due to their pure nature, the conviction that there is a Creator, Master and Caretaker of this universe is implanted in their hearts very early in their lives and they remain constantly in search of His guidance and help, as the Holy Quran mentions:

لَئِن لَّمْ يَهْدِنِى رَبِّى لَأَكُونَنَّ مِنَ ٱلْقَوْمِ ٱلضَّآلِّينَ

> Unless my Lord guides me, I will surely be among the people gone astray. [Al-An'am, 6:77]

The effect of the purity of their heart is that every object of this world appears temporary and transitory to them. They have no deception that everything of the universe - including the stars, moon and sun - is destined to perish. Thus they do not fall in love with them. They instinctively speak out as Prophet Ibrahim (*alaihis salaam*) declared:

لَآ أُحِبُّ ٱلْآفِلِينَ

> I like not those which disappear. [Al-An'am, 6:76]

They continue to search for the Living, the Self-Subsisting, and the Eternal. And when they find Him, they cannot sit, but declare immediately:

إِنِّى بَرِىٓءٌ مِّمَّا تُشْرِكُونَ (78) إِنِّى وَجَّهْتُ وَجْهِىَ لِلَّذِى فَطَرَ ٱلسَّمَٰوَٰتِ وَٱلْأَرْضَ حَنِيفًا وَمَآ أَنَا۠ مِنَ ٱلْمُشْرِكِينَ (79)

> I am indeed free from your (guilt) of associating partners to Allah. For me, I have set my face, firmly and truly, towards Him Who created the heavens and the earth, and never shall I associate partners to Allah. [Al-An'am, 6:78-79]

A prophet's heart is pure. It has no room for anything other than Allah and it is completely free from the influence of everything else. This is the kind of heart Prophet Ibrahim (*alaihis salaam*) possessed, as the Holy Quran says:

وَلَقَدْ ءَاتَيْنَا إِبْرَاهِيمَ رُشْدَهُ مِن قَبْلُ وَكُنَّا بِهِ عَالِمِينَ

Surely We had bestowed wisdom upon Ibrahim even earlier, and We knew him well. [Al-Anbiya, 21:51]

وَإِنَّ مِن شِيعَتِهِ لَإِبْرَاهِيمَ (83) إِذْ جَاءَ رَبَّهُ بِقَلْبٍ سَلِيمٍ (84) إِذْ قَالَ لِأَبِيهِ وَقَوْمِهِ مَاذَا تَعْبُدُونَ (85) أَئِفْكًا ءَالِهَةً دُونَ اللَّهِ تُرِيدُونَ (86) فَمَا ظَنُّكُم بِرَبِّ الْعَالَمِينَ (87)

Ibrahim was of the same faith. He came to his Lord with a sound heart. He said to his father and to his people, "Behold! What are these which you worship? Are you serving false deities instead of God? What do you think of the Lord of the worlds?" [As-Saffat, 37:83-87]

Though prophets possessed the best of intelligence, acumen and ability, they did not engage themselves in acquiring or advancing the knowledge or skill that was in vogue at their time. Instead they kept themselves fully and exclusively engaged in the very task for which they were sent into this world – the task of making people aware of their Creator and what He wants from them.

Prophetic Teachings compared to other Types of Knowledge

How is the knowledge of prophets different from that of others? Here is an example to illustrate the difference.

Once a few students were riding in a boat and enjoying the ride. For the sake of fun, they started joking with the boatman who was an uneducated old fellow. One student said to the boatman, "O Uncle! Which subjects have you studied?" The boatman replied, "I have not studied anything." The student said, "Did you study science?" The boatman said, "I don't know even its name." Another student said, "How about algebra and trigonometry?" The boatman said, "These names are new to me." The third student said, "Then, you must have studied history and geography." The boatman said, "Are these the names of places or people?"

The students could not control their laughter. Then they asked the boatman, "How old are you?" The boatman replied, "Around forty years." Upon that the students said, "You have wasted half of your life by not studying anything." The boatman felt demoralized and kept quiet.

After a short time, a violent storm broke out at the sea, waves started riding high, the boat began rocking and a scene of death and disaster began to unravel. This was the first such experience for those students. They became very nervous and panicked.

The boatman asked the students, "Which subjects have you studied?" Upon that they mentioned all the subjects that they had studied in their schools and colleges.

The boatman then asked, "That is well and good, but have you learned swimming? If the boat capsizes, how are you going to swim to the shore?"

Unfortunately, none of the students had learned swimming. They said very sadly, "Uncle! This is the only thing that we did not learn."

The boatman laughed at that and said, "I lost only half of my life, but you may now lose all of your life. In this storm, none of the subjects that you have studied so far will be of any use. The only thing that can save your life today is swimming which you did not learn."

Not knowing how to swim is a sure way to drown. Not taking a life-saving elixir is a sure way to die. Likewise, not accepting the teachings of prophets is a sure way (for a nation) to fail and vanish. History is full of evidence to testify that the nations which disparaged and ignored the teachings of their prophets were ultimately disgraced and destroyed.

Divine Knowledge

It is divine knowledge that makes man aware of his real worth and leads him to real success. It is this knowledge which enables him to recognize the Creator of the universe and His attributes; his own beginning and end; his position in the universe and his relationship with the Creator. It is this knowledge which makes him aware of what pleases Allah; what displeases Him; what makes him successful or unsuccessful in the Hereafter; what the rewards and punishments of his deeds are; and what his conduct should be.

It is this knowledge which keeps a man on the right path, enables him to discipline and control his carnal desires, makes him aware of the consequences of his actions, motivates him to do good deeds and refrain from evil deeds, and prods him to prepare for the Life Hereafter.

It is this knowledge which creates the fear of Allah in the hearts of people. It brings into existence a modest and chaste society. It ensures the protection of human civilization. It makes a person stay away from selfishness and arrogance. It frees a person from lust and greed of this world. It prevents a person from engaging in vain and useless pursuits. It enables a person to lead a moderate and balanced life.

Libraries and encyclopedias of philosophers and thinkers are empty of divine knowledge. Philosophers and thinkers have no knowledge of the Life Hereafter which prophets are able to describe so vividly. The entire effort of philosophers and thinkers is geared towards this life and they cannot see anything that pertains to the life after death, as the Holy Quran has mentioned:

يَعْلَمُونَ ظَـٰهِرًا مِّنَ ٱلْحَيَوٰةِ ٱلدُّنْيَا وَهُمْ عَنِ ٱلْأَخِرَةِ هُمْ غَـٰفِلُونَ

They know only the outside appearance of the life of this world, but they are heedless of the Hereafter. [Ar-Rum, 30:7]

بَلِ ٱدَّارَكَ عِلْمُهُمْ فِى ٱلْأَخِرَةِ ۚ بَلْ هُمْ فِى شَكٍّ مِّنْهَا ۖ بَلْ هُم مِّنْهَا عَمُونَ

> Still less do they comprehend the life to come. In fact they
> are in doubt about it. Still more, they are blind to it. [An-
> Naml, 27:66]

Those nations which depended solely upon their own knowledge, discoveries and inventions and ignored divine teachings of the prophets of their time were doomed forever. The Holy Quran states:

$$\text{فَلَمَّا جَاءَتْهُمْ رُسُلُهُم بِٱلْبَيِّنَٰتِ فَرِحُوا بِمَا عِندَهُم مِّنَ ٱلْعِلْمِ وَحَاقَ بِهِم مَّا كَانُوا بِهِ يَسْتَهْزِءُونَ}$$

> When their messengers came to them with manifest signs,
> they gloated because of the knowledge they had, but they
> were ultimately encircled by what they used to ridicule.
> [Ghafir, 40:83]

The same rule applies to the nations of today as well. Since Prophet Muhammad (saw) came as the final prophet, he is the prophet for all the people and all the eras until the Last Day. Thus the progress and survival of all the nations who are living on the earth today or will be coming in future depend solely on following the teachings of Prophet Muhammad (saw).

D'awah of Prophets

After a prophet has witnessed the reality that this universe is created by Allah, He is its sole Master and Sustainer and all other creations of the universe have fully surrendered to Him, he is astonished to see why man is so reluctant in submitting to Allah despite belonging to the same universe.

The stark reality is that man is unwittingly in submission to Allah due to his unlimited dependence on Him for all of his needs – in his birth, in his sustenance, in his growth from childhood to youth and from youth to old age, in his sickness and cure and in whatever he eats and drinks. But when he is asked to openly declare his surrender to Allah, he is reluctant to do so.

Some people go even further than that and start worshipping and bowing before creations like themselves. Seeing that, prophets used to spontaneously say, as the Holy Quran mentions:

$$\text{أَفَغَيْرَ دِينِ ٱللَّهِ يَبْغُونَ وَلَهُ أَسْلَمَ مَن فِى ٱلسَّمَـٰوَٰتِ وَٱلْأَرْضِ}$$
$$\text{طَوْعًا وَكَرْهًا وَإِلَيْهِ يُرْجَعُونَ}$$

Do they seek a religion other than that of Allah while all creatures in the heavens and on the earth have, willingly or unwillingly, bowed to His Will, and to Him shall they all be brought back. [Al-Imran, 3:83]

The Holy Quran has repeatedly mentioned the humility and subservience of the creations, as in the following verse:

$$\text{وَلِلَّهِ يَسْجُدُ مَا فِى ٱلسَّمَـٰوَٰتِ وَمَا فِى ٱلْأَرْضِ مِن دَآبَّةٍ}$$
$$\text{وَٱلْمَلَـٰئِكَةُ وَهُمْ لَا يَسْتَكْبِرُونَ (49) يَخَافُونَ رَبَّهُم مِّن فَوْقِهِم}$$
$$\text{وَيَفْعَلُونَ مَا يُؤْمَرُونَ (50)}$$

And to Allah prostrates whatever is in the heavens and whatever is on the earth and the angels [as well], and they are not arrogant. They fear their Lord above them, and they do what they are commanded. [An-Nahl, 16:49-50]

Prophets invited people to submit wholeheartedly to the One to whom everything else of the universe is in full submission. They invited people to live a life that is in accordance with the orders of the Creator of the earth and skies, give up all of their vain desires, concede all of their freedom, renounce all of their ownership and fully surrender themselves to the Almighty. This is what Islam is all about and this has been the message of every prophet.

After a person has understood that he has to ultimately return to Allah and give account of his deeds to Him, he cannot become heedless and oblivious. He will not live a life as he pleases. He will live a life as the Almighty Allah desires and all of his activities - personal, political, social and otherwise - will be dictated by His orders.

Man may ignore divine revelations and prophetic teachings and assume that he is different from all other creations of the universe. He may think that he is not governed by any super being and he is not accountable to anyone after this life. This is the path of utter ignorance and forgetfulness. It is like establishing tiny rebellious states in the vast kingdom of Allah.

Foundation of a Robust Society

A human society is not made of mortar, bricks, paper and cotton; nor is it a vehicle of skillfully fulfilling vain desires. It is a venue of shared living in which the system of nature is established, every individual gets his due share and people are able to fulfill their responsibilities and achieve the desired purpose of life.

Prophets bring to mankind the skill, framework and guidelines which can bring into existence a society that is chaste, pious, fair and just. They are like the gardeners of this world. They maintain flowers and trees and remove weeds and thorns. Any society that grows without their guidance is like a wild tree which is full of defects and grows into a thorny and bitter tree unable to provide shade or sweet fruit.

Prophets are enlightened with the reality of nature. They also know the psyche of man. A society that is not founded on their teachings will always remain unbalanced. The more that society advances, the more its shortcomings and deficiencies are exposed. That is why we find that all the major civilizations of the world experienced their greatest levels of social upheaval and moral decay at the time of their zenith of glory and power. During their peak period, weaknesses and failings of their system became exposed; marital and family life became unstable; injustice and corruption became widespread; and the society as a whole became chaotic and immoral. Ultimately those ailments forced such societies to crumble and dissipate. It is as if the periods of glory and destruction overlap each other.

It may not be obvious to many, but it is a fact that *'aqeedah* (faith) - religious, social or cultural - has always provided a solid foundation to sustained civilizations. A civilization that is not founded on a set of beliefs is invariably flimsy and unstable.

Prophets bring correct *'aqeedah* which in turn develops in people qualities and traits upon which the structure of a sound and durable civilization may be built.

There were nations, which either unknowingly or by choice, chose not to lay their foundation on divine revelations and prophetic teachings; there were also those which were initially established upon such teachings but later drifted away from them. Those nations in reality did not accept anything that was beyond their physical discernment and chose to be guided only by their own intuitions, observations and experiences. Their views of morality and standards of right and wrong kept on changing continuously. Their ethics and ideals vacillated constantly. What was right today was declared wrong tomorrow. What was not permissible today was made permissible tomorrow. What was tyranny today was classified as an act of justice tomorrow.

Those societies lost the sense of right and wrong, good and bad, virtue and evil. In the guise of freedom, lawlessness, chaos and confusion thrived. Moral and ethical anarchy became order of the day. Life became miserable. Peace and security became rare. Such societies became a terrible scourge for the rest of the world.

A study of the history of various cultures and civilizations makes it obvious that their downfall and ultimate destruction occurred when they wavered in their commitment to religious and moral principles, manipulated moral and ethical standards and compromised with nature's value system.

National pride and cultural traditions were able to sustain them only for a short period of time before they were completely taken over and annihilated by moral anarchy and social upheaval. To justify and put a positive face on moral decay and social disorder, new ideas and philosophies are often advanced. But they do very little to save the society from reaching a state in which it completely severs its relationship from the laws of nature and loses the ability to distinguish between right and wrong.

Without prophetic teachings and divine revelations, life becomes purely materialistic. People start believing that they are just like other animals except that they can speak. This belief and conviction degrades them to such an extent that the fulfillment of physical needs and desires becomes the sole objective of their lives.

Effects of Prophetic Teachings

It is only the prophets who inform us about our superiority over other creations and about our real worth and status. They also enlighten us with the knowledge that we are under the command of a Supreme Being; we are accountable to Him for all of our actions; this universe belongs to Him; all the dwellers of this universe are His subject; and we are not totally free in utilizing the resources of this universe or in dealing with fellow human beings and other creations.

Not only do they develop the sense of right and wrong among humans, but they also provide a complete code of conduct. They inform humans about the rewards which Allah has promised for good deeds and punishment for bad deeds. No other incentive has proven more powerful and effective in motivating a person to do virtuous deeds and refrain from evil deeds.

They ingrain in the hearts and minds of people the conviction that Allah sees everything, hears everything and knows everything, seen or unseen. This is the most powerful tool that has ever been discovered to discipline human behavior. It is this force which keeps a man in check in both broad daylight and the darkest of nights. It is this power which makes him follow the law in the city as well as in the desert. It is this strength which enables him to forsake an evil to which he may be addicted for years. It is the key to eradicating crimes from society without deploying police or army. It is so powerful that a short announcement was enough to make the entire community quit drinking alcohol without any hesitation[3]. It is so powerful that the wrongdoers confessed their crimes and flocked on their own to the court of law for punishment.

The society which is deprived of the divine system and moral conscience stands on the brink of disaster despite its materialistic, educational, industrial and political advancements. In fact, these advancements accelerate the decline and destruction of the society which is ripe in immorality and ignorance towards the Creator. Such a society plays in the hands of Satan and uses its influence and resources to promote evil and immorality by condemning traditional moral values and legitimizing illicit acts of indecency and lewdness. The ancient Greek and Roman empires and the modern society of today are good examples of the same.

The moral and ethical system which is devoid of prophetic teachings is merely a hollow philosophy that fails to eradicate even a single vice or to establish even a tiny island of righteousness and piety[4].

---

[3] It refers to the divine order that came in Madinah for the prohibition of alcohol.

[4] The National prohibition of alcohol (1920-33) of the United States of America offers a good example of the fallacy of such a system. The prohibition law (known as the Eighteenth Amendment to the Constitution) banning the sale, production, and transportation of alcohol was enacted in 1920 to reduce crime and corruption, solve social problems, reduce the tax burden created by prisons and poorhouses, and improve health and hygiene in America. But it proved to be a failed social and political experiment and law enforcement nightmare. Although consumption of alcohol fell at the beginning of Prohibition, it subsequently increased. Alcohol

Divine Laws versus Man-made Laws

Divine laws have the ability to rein man's reckless freedom. But man, instead of accepting and obeying those laws, tends to take charge of framing laws in his hands. And since the laws which he makes are based upon his limited knowledge and experience and are mostly dictated by either majority opinion or greed of power, he in reality removes all the constraints which could have stopped him from going astray.

Man is by nature overwhelmed by lust, desires and temptations. He likes to remain free from any restriction. He loves ease, comfort and luxury. If he does not have the fear of Allah and is not conscious about his responsibilities, what is there to force him to pass laws that will curb his freedom, restrict his behavior and curtail his fun and amusement? What can be expected of those who have been brought up with mistaken belief, confused thinking and distorted ideology? How can they be expected to pass laws which will not tolerate and promote profanity and sinful acts? They will in fact use their influence and power to pass laws to legitimize immoral and indecent acts.[5]

History tells us that there were nations which passed laws to legalize illicit and abhorrent acts and there were others who outlawed chastity and drove chaste people out of their homes into exile, as the Holy Quran has mentioned:

$$ أَخْرِجُوٓاْ ءَالَ لُوطٍ مِّن قَرْيَتِكُمْ إِنَّهُمْ أُنَاسٌ يَتَطَهَّرُونَ $$

---

became more dangerous to consume; crime increased and became "organized"; the court and prison systems were stretched to the breaking point; and corruption of public officials was rampant. No measurable gains were made in productivity or reduced absenteeism. Prohibition removed a significant source of tax revenue and greatly increased government spending. It led many drinkers to switch to opium, marijuana, patent medicines, cocaine, and other dangerous substances which they would have not gone to in the absence of Prohibition.
The Prohibition law was ultimately repealed (known as the Twenty-first Amendment to the Constitution) in 1933.
[5] There have been several instances in recent past that the acts which have been considered illegitimate throughout human history have been granted legal status. For example, before the Nazi period in Germany, homosexuality was declared permissible if the parties involved had consented or in case of a minor, permission was granted by the guardian. Syed Abu 'Ala Maududi has cited several instances in his book entitled *Purdah*.

> Drive out the followers of Lut from your city; these are indeed men who want to be clean and pure! [An-Naml, 27:56]

The society which is founded on prophetic teachings does not give power to man to make laws. In such a society, a man upon breaking a law and committing a sin has to bear the punishment. But he is not allowed to fiddle with the divine laws and make changes to them. The laws of *Shari'ah* mandate what is *halaal* (permissible) and what is *haraam* (forbidden) and are immutable like the laws of nature and the course of the sun and moon, as the Holy Quran says:

$$\text{فِطْرَتَ ٱللَّهِ ٱلَّتِى فَطَرَ ٱلنَّاسَ عَلَيْهَا ۚ لَا تَبْدِيلَ لِخَلْقِ ٱللَّهِ ۚ ذَٰلِكَ ٱلدِّينُ ٱلْقَيِّمُ}$$

> Allah has created man on the nature that He has designed. There is no change in Allah's creation. That is the straight religion. [Ar-Rum, 30:30]

Neither the laws of nature nor the temperament of man will ever change. That is why all the immoral, lustful, sinful and criminal acts which are outlawed by divine laws will remain prohibited forever.

The basic purpose of the laws which humans make is to ensure that the administration runs smoothly and people live peacefully. That is why lawmakers take into consideration only those aspects of human behavior which affect social and public life and do not worry about the personal and private lives of individuals. These laws act more like policemen than reformers.

But the divine laws seek much more than merely establishing a smoothly running administration. They also aim at making people pious and god-fearing. That is why they may disallow certain things which may not seem important to human lawmakers. They constrict everything that has the potential of instigating and incubating evil, immorality, lewdness, lustfulness, luxuriousness and criminal attitude. They disallow everything that promotes vices which may attack and destroy the very foundation of a society, like termites do to a building. They do not encourage music, fun and amusement. They do not promote pomp, show and fashion. They do not endorse and encourage competition in accumulation of wealth and worldly possessions. They discourage building huge structures for show and splendor. They prohibit use of utensils made of gold and silver. They prohibit use of silk and gold for men. They prohibit images and statues of humans and animals.

In a man-made system, the only deterrent to committing a wrong is the fear of being caught by police. If that fear is absent, there is nothing else that can stop a person from going against the law.

It is also a fact that people do not have genuine respect for man-made laws because they know that these laws have been made by humans like themselves. Those who become in-charge of making laws usually reach that position by means of their political clout, wealth or influence and they are not necessarily better than others in morality or character. Elected officials are often worse than the general public in abusing power and wealth; they are more corrupt, dishonest and crooked than a common man. The lawmakers often make and amend laws for their own personal gains or to cover up their wrongdoings. That is why public is often reluctant to accept the laws or amendments which are legislated by elected officials and many try to evade them, either openly or through loopholes.

On the other hand, divine laws which come in the form of revelations and prophetic teachings command utmost respect in the hearts of those who believe in the Creator and His prophets. They consider those laws to be as sacred as the prophets and divine scriptures. To them, trying to evade or circumvent those laws is an act of treason, as the Holy Quran says:

وَٱلَّذِينَ سَعَوْ فِى ءَايَـٰتِنَا مُعَـٰجِزِينَ أُوْلَـٰٓئِكَ لَهُمْ عَذَابٌ مِّن رِّجْزٍ أَلِيمٌ

> For those who strive against Our signs to defeat them, there is a painful punishment of the divine wrath. [Saba, 34:5]

It is not enough to observe the laws only externally and physically. They must also be followed in spirit because the Supreme Commander of the law knows everything, whether it is open or secret, and He cannot be deceived like the authorities of this world, as the Holy Quran says:

لَن يَنَالَ ٱللَّهَ لُحُومُهَا وَلَا دِمَآؤُهَا وَلَـٰكِن يَنَالُهُ ٱلتَّقْوَىٰ مِنكُمْ

> It is not the meat or blood that reaches Allah; it is your piety that reaches Him. [Al-Hajj, 22:37]

What impact will such laws have on the society? What will be the level of piety, uprightness, chastity, modesty, humility, honesty and civility in society as a result of the application of such laws?

When the administration of a locality will come in the hands of those who possess unshakable belief in divine laws and have been raised in an environment which is free from worldly lust and greed, will the result be any different from what the Holy Quran has predicted:

$$\text{ٱلَّذِينَ إِن مَّكَّنَّـٰهُمْ فِى ٱلْأَرْضِ أَقَامُواْ ٱلصَّلَوٰةَ وَءَاتَوُاْ ٱلزَّكَوٰةَ وَأَمَرُواْ بِٱلْمَعْرُوفِ وَنَهَوْاْ عَنِ ٱلْمُنكَرِ}$$

> They are those who, if We establish them in the land, will establish regular prayer and give regular charity, enjoin the right and forbid the wrong. [Al-Hajj, 24:41]

Can there be any doubt about the sanctity and serenity of the society that will come into existence under the command of such people?

On the other hand, what will be the condition of the society whose architects are ignorant of divine teachings; do not have sound belief; do not have a clear mission in life; do not have well-defined rules to determine right and wrong; continue changing the rules of ethics and morality; make rules to suit their own convenience and use power and authority for personal gains? Will man be able to fulfill the mission of his life and reach his full potential in such a society? Such a society will be human in name only and people will behave like lifeless machines. People will have no feeling or concern for others and will act like wild animals.

What Prophets Gave to Mankind

Prophets not only provided mankind with the recognition of the Creator and the knowledge of the Life Hereafter, but they also provided what is most needed for the development and progress of human society - motivation for good deeds, aversion for evil deeds, resolve to fight *shirk* and enthusiasm to strive and sacrifice for the promotion of good, etc. These are the main forces which enable humans to reach the highest level of achievement.

When people abandoned good qualities, prophets came and worked tirelessly to revive those qualities. They worked hard to nurture in people an affinity for virtue, aversion for evil, and ability to stand firm in supporting truth and opposing falsehood. They nurtured the quality of mercy and tolerance to replace injustice and cruelty. They developed the quality of generosity, humility and modesty and elevated people to the highest level of morality and decency.

The result of their tireless efforts and unparalleled sacrifices was that savage people changed into decent human beings. There came into existence such individuals who exceeded angels in piety and devotion. Humanity got a new lease on life. Justice prevailed and the weaker section of society did not fear in demanding its rights from the oppressors. Wolves were able to shepherd lambs. The whole atmosphere overflowed with mercy and kindness. Love and affection became abundant. Goodness prevailed everywhere. The world turned into a garden of Paradise. People freed themselves from the slavery of lust and desire. Hearts became tender and were attracted to good deeds like iron particles are attracted to magnet.

Prophets are in reality the torchbearers of nobility and good character and mankind is most heavily indebted to them. They are the saviors of humanity. Had they not come, humanity would have perished despite all of its knowledge, philosophy, culture, civilization and advancements. Had they not come, humans would have lived in this world like wild animals without knowing their creator and purpose of their life. Man would have known nothing except eating, drinking and fulfilling his desires.

Whatever good we see today in the world - high moral values, good manners, noble ideas, beneficial knowledge, and courage to fight evil, etc. – comes from the divine revelations and teachings of prophets. The world will remain indebted to prophets forever for their courage, perseverance and sacrifices in bringing enlightenment to mankind. It is only their shadow under which humanity has ever prospered in past and it is only their guidance and teachings which can bring success to humanity in future.

Perseverance and Commitment of Prophets

The commitment of prophets to the divine message which they received from Allah was absolutely firm and uncompromising. They were not willing to alter or modify that message at any cost to make it more appealing and attractive to people. The Holy Quran mentions their determination in the following verses:

$$\text{فَٱصۡدَعۡ بِمَا تُؤۡمَرُ وَأَعۡرِضۡ عَنِ ٱلۡمُشۡرِكِينَ}$$

Therefore expound openly what you are commanded, and turn away from those who join false gods with Allah. [Al-Hijr, 15:94]

$$\text{يَـٰٓأَيُّهَا ٱلرَّسُولُ بَلِّغۡ مَآ أُنزِلَ إِلَيۡكَ مِن رَّبِّكَۖ وَإِن لَّمۡ تَفۡعَلۡ فَمَا بَلَّغۡتَ رِسَالَتَهُۥۚ وَٱللَّهُ يَعۡصِمُكَ مِنَ ٱلنَّاسِ}$$

O Messenger! Proclaim the (message) which has been sent to you from your Lord. If you did not, you would not have fulfilled and proclaimed His mission. And Allah will defend you from men (who mean mischief). [Al-Maidah, 5:67]

$$\text{وَدُّواْ لَوۡ تُدۡهِنُ فَيُدۡهِنُونَ}$$

They wish that you would soften [in your position], so they would also soften [toward you]. [Al-Qalam, 68:9]

For example, the stand of Prophet Muhammad (saw) on *Tawheed* and other fundamentals including obligatory prayers was unequivocal and unbending. After the conquest of Makkah and Taif (a city 60 miles away from Makkah) in 8th Hijri (630 AD), when the people of Thaqif tribe (inhabitants of Taif) came to the Prophet (saw) to enter into the fold of Islam, their delegation insisted that their idol Al-Lat[6] not be dismantled and they be allowed to maintain their allegiance to the idol for the next three years.

The Prophet (saw) categorically rejected their condition. They then asked that they be allowed to maintain their allegiance to Al-Lat for two years and the Prophet rejected it as well. They then asked for one year and the Prophet rejected it too. Finally they asked for one month. In response to that, the Prophet dispatched Abu Sufyan bin Harb (who had some relatives in Taif) and Mughirah bin Sh'obah (who was from the tribe of Thaqif) to go to Taif and dismantle the idol of Al-Lat.

---

[6] Al-Lat was the most revered idol after the idols of Makkah and it was this idol which gave Taif its status as the most revered place second only to Makkah.

The delegation had also requested the Prophet (saw) that they be exempted from the obligatory prayers. The Prophet responded, "There is no *khair*[7] (goodness) in the religion which has no obligatory prayers."

The delegation then returned to Taif. Abu Sufyan bin Harb and Mughirah bin Sh'obah also went with them and dismantled the idol of Al-Lat. Soon thereafter, the entire tribe of Thaqif entered into the fold of Islam. This was the result of the Prophet's unshakable commitment to his mission.

Method of Prophets' *D'awah*

Prophets passionately invited people towards Allah and the Life Hereafter. They gave glad tidings of the bounties of Paradise and warned about the horrors of Hell. They used to describe details of Paradise and Hell as if they were witnessing them with their own eyes. They used to ask people to believe in *ghaib* (unseen) unconditionally without getting into philosophical and hypothetical arguments. Their *d'awah* (invitation) was straightforward and they did not waver in enforcing the orders of Allah.

1. Straightforwardness

When a prophet came to a land, there were certain arts, skills, trades, ideas and philosophies which were very popular there at that time, but he did not use them to make his invitation more attractive and appealing to people. He invited people in a straightforward manner to believe in Allah, His powers and attributes, angels, *qadr*[8] (destiny) and resurrection. He was unapologetic in declaring that the reward of believing in his message was Paradise and the pleasure of Allah.

The incident known as the Second 'Aqabah Pledge which took place in the 13th year (622 AD) of the prophethood of Prophet Muhammad (saw) offers an excellent example in this regard.

A group of 73 men and two women came from Madinah to Makkah for *hajj*. They were staying in the valley of 'Aqabah. The Prophet (saw) came to them with his uncle 'Abbas bin 'Abdul Muttalib (who had not entered Islam yet), recited a few verses of the Holy Quran and invited them towards Allah and Islam. Upon that they accepted Islam.

---

[7] خیر

[8] قدر

The Prophet (saw) then said to them, "Pledge that you will protect me as you protect your family." They took the pledge and the Prophet pledged back to them that he would never desert them and would not go back to his own people.

The men from Madinah were very astute and intelligent. They knew fully well the ramifications of the pledge which they had made to the Prophet (saw). They knew very well that they were inviting animosity and hostility not only from their own tribe, but from all the Arab tribes. When 'Abbas bin 'Abadah Ansari (who was one of them) reminded them of the ensuing hardship, they all said in one voice, "We know what we are getting into. We are willing to risk our lives, the lives of our dear ones and our possessions." They then turned to the Prophet (saw) and asked, "What are we going to get if we fulfill our pledge?"

At such a critical juncture, if there was a political leader in place of a prophet, he would have probably said: You will gain strength and you will be recognized as a formidable force in the entire Arab world.

Such a promise (of becoming a formidable force) was not totally unrealistic as the signs pointing in that direction had already started emerging. For example, one of the men who had come from Madinah had already remarked to the Prophet (saw), "Our tribe is divided and shattered like no other tribe. We hope that Allah will unite them due to your blessing. We will now go and present to them your *d'awah* which we have accepted. If Allah unites them because of you, no one will be more dignified and powerful than you."

But the Prophet (saw) in reply to their question simply said, "Paradise." He did not promise anything of this world and he was not at all apologetic in doing so. The entire delegation then took the pledge of allegiance at his hands.

2. Strict Enforcement of Divine Laws

It is also a special quality of prophets that they do not tolerate any alteration or compromise in enforcing the orders of *Shari'ah*. They do not delay or discard the implementation of any divine order. They enforce the order whether it affects one of their own or someone else.

A woman of the tribe of Makhzum was found guilty of stealing[9]. Osama bin Zaid (ra), who was very dear to the Prophet (saw), approached the Prophet on her behalf for leniency. The Prophet became very angry and said, "Do you intercede regarding one of the punishments prescribed by Allah?" and addressed the people, "People before you were destroyed because when someone from the upper echelon of the society committed a theft, they spared him, but when someone belonging to a low class committed a theft, they inflicted the prescribed punishment upon him. By Allah, if Fatima, the daughter of Muhammad, were to steal, I would not hesitate in getting her hands cut off."

This is the kind of character that Prophet Muhammad (saw) had inculcated in his illustrious Companions. They followed the edicts of the Holy Quran and *Shari'ah* without looking at the consequences and upheld the principles of Islam in every situation. The incident which took place with Jabla bin Aiham Al-Ghassani during the caliphate of 'Umar bin Khattab (the 2nd caliph) stands as a glowing example in this regard.

Jabla bin Aiham Al-Ghassani was the king of a small state near Syria. He was originally a Christian, but later embraced Islam. He came to Madinah with 500 people during the caliphate of 'Umar (ra). He had such a lavish lifestyle that when he entered Madinah, there was not a single individual, including women, who did not come out to watch his splendor.

When 'Umar (ra) went to Makkah for *hajj*, Jabla also accompanied him. While Jabla was performing *tawaaf*[10] (circumambulation) around the K'aba, a man from the tribe of Fazzarah inadvertently stepped on Jabla's robe which became untied. Jabla became very furious and slapped the man on his face. The man complained to 'Umar (ra) upon which 'Umar (ra) summoned Jabla. When 'Umar (ra) asked Jabla about the incident, Jabla said, "The man attempted to untie my robe. Was it not for the sanctity of K'aba, I would have hit him on his face with my sword." 'Umar (ra) said to him, "Since you have confessed your fault, you have to ask the man to forgive you. Or, I will have to extract *qisas*[11] (compensation) from you." Jabla asked 'Umar (ra), "What will you do with me for *qisas*?" 'Umar (ra) said, "I will ask the man to hit you as you had hit him."

---

[9] Reported in *Sahih Muslim, Kitab al-Hudud.*
[10] طواف
[11] قصاص

Jabla was stunned to hear that. He said to 'Umar (ra), "How can it be so? He is an ordinary person and I am an honorable man of my tribe and locality." 'Umar (ra) said, "Islam has made him and you equal. You cannot be better than him except on the basis of *taqwa[12]* (piety)." Jabla said, "I had hoped that my acceptance of Islam would elevate my status and position." 'Umar (ra) said to him, "Forget about it. You have to get the man ready to forgive you. Or, get ready to pay *qisas*."

When Jabla saw 'Umar (ra) unflinching in his decision, he asked 'Umar (ra) that he be given time to think about it overnight. 'Umar (ra) agreed to his request. When it became dark and everyone went to sleep, Jabla took his horses and camels and escaped towards Syria. Upon reaching Syria, Jabla abandoned Islam.

After a long time, Jathaama bin Masahiq (a Companion of the Prophet) happened to visit Jabla. After his return from Syria, when Jathaama bin Masahiq described the luxury and splendor of Jabla's court, 'Umar (ra) remarked, "He is a loser. He bought this world in lieu of the Hereafter."

Wisdom of *D'awah*

Prophets used the best wisdom in their *d'awah* and utilized the approach that was most suitable for the psyche and level of understanding of the audience. If it was not so, their effort would have conflicted with what the Holy Quran has prescribed in many of its verses. The Holy Quran says:

$$\text{وَمَآ أَرْسَلْنَا مِن رَّسُولٍ إِلَّا بِلِسَانِ قَوْمِهِ لِيُبَيِّنَ لَهُمْ}$$

And We did not send any messenger except [speaking] in the language of his people to state clearly for them. [Ibrahim, 14:4]

The language does not mean merely a collection of words and sentences. It also includes the mode, style and strategy of getting a message across. The best examples are found in the conversations that Prophet Yusuf[13] (*alaihis salaam*) had with his two co-prisoners and those which Prophet Ibrahim

---

[12] تقوی
[13] Known as Joseph in Western literature

(*alaihis salaam*) and Prophet Musa[14] (*alaihis salaam*) had with the respective kings of their time.

In the following verse of the Holy Quran, Allah has instructed Prophet Muhammad (saw) and all of his followers about how they should convey the message:

$$ادْعُ إِلَىٰ سَبِيلِ رَبِّكَ بِالْحِكْمَةِ وَالْمَوْعِظَةِ الْحَسَنَةِ وَجَادِلْهُم بِالَّتِي هِيَ أَحْسَنُ$$

> Invite to the way of your Lord with wisdom and good instruction, and argue with them in a way that is best. [An-Nahl, 16:125]

When the Prophet (saw) used to send his Companions on any mission, he used to instruct them to be soft, tolerant and forgiving to people and to give them glad tidings. When he sent Mu'adh bin Jabal (ra) and Abu Musa Ash'ari (ra) to Yemen, he told them, "Make things easy for people, do not make things difficult for them, give them glad tidings and do not scare them." [*Sahih Bukhari, Book of Al-Maghaazi*]

Allah Himself has mentioned about the Prophet (saw):

$$فَبِمَا رَحْمَةٍ مِّنَ اللَّهِ لِنتَ لَهُمْ ۖ وَلَوْ كُنتَ فَظًّا غَلِيظَ الْقَلْبِ لَانفَضُّوا مِنْ حَوْلِكَ$$

> It is part of the Mercy of Allah that you deal gently with them. Were you severe or harsh-hearted, they would have broken away from you. [Al-Imran, 3:159]

The Prophet (saw) used to tell his Companions, "You have been sent to make things easy for people. You have not been sent to make things difficult for them."

There are numerous verses of the Holy Quran and countless incidents which support this approach. This had been the practice of previous prophets as well. After enumerating the accomplishments of various prophets, the Holy Quran says:

---

[14] Known as Moses in Western literature

$$\text{أُوْلَـٰئِكَ ٱلَّذِينَ ءَاتَيْنَـٰهُمُ ٱلْكِتَـٰبَ وَٱلْحُكْمَ وَٱلنُّبُوَّةَ}$$

These were the men to whom We gave the book, authority, and prophethood. [Al-An'am, 6:89]

But it should be understood that leniency and accommodation was allowed only in peripheral matters and not in *'aqeedah* and core principles. All the prophets were absolutely firm and uncompromising in matters pertaining to *'aqeedah* and core principles.

Emphasis of Quran on Following Prophets

The Holy Quran frequently urges believers to follow the ways and lifestyle of prophets, as in the following verse:

$$\text{لَّقَدْ كَانَ لَكُمْ فِى رَسُولِ ٱللَّهِ أُسْوَةٌ حَسَنَةٌ لِّمَن كَانَ يَرْجُواْ ٱللَّهَ}$$
$$\text{وَٱلْيَوْمَ ٱلْءَاخِرَ وَذَكَرَ ٱللَّهَ كَثِيرًا}$$

You have indeed in the Messenger of Allah a beautiful pattern (of conduct) for anyone whose hope is in Allah and the Final Day, and who engages much in the Praise of Allah. [Al-Ahzab, 33:21]

It instructs them to constantly seek Allah's guidance by reciting the following *d'ua*[15] (supplication):

$$\text{ٱهْدِنَا ٱلصِّرَٰطَ ٱلْمُسْتَقِيمَ (6) صِرَٰطَ ٱلَّذِينَ أَنْعَمْتَ عَلَيْهِمْ غَيْرِ}$$
$$\text{ٱلْمَغْضُوبِ عَلَيْهِمْ وَلَا ٱلضَّآلِّينَ (7)}$$

Guide us to the straight path, the path of those upon whom You have bestowed Your favor, not of those who have evoked Your anger or of those who have gone astray. [Al-Fatihah, 1:6-7]

Prophets are undoubtedly the most blessed group of people and they are the ones whom we ought to follow. That is why it has been made

---

[15] دعا

obligatory for Muslims to recite the above *d'ua* in every *rak'ah*[16] (unit) of *salah*[17] (prayer).

If a person truly fulfills the requirements of this *d'ua* and earnestly strives to follow the footsteps of the blessed ones, he will certainly gain nearness to Allah and become dear to Him.

Love and Respect for Prophets

The Holy Quran calls for utmost love and respect for prophets, the kind of love that is intense and deeply rooted in hearts. It is not enough to obey them just for the sake of obeying. They should be obeyed and followed with utmost passion and enthusiasm. The relationship between prophets and their followers should not be like what usually exists between a king and his subjects or between a political or military leader and his followers.

The Holy Quran does not deem it sufficient for Muslims to fulfill obligations such as the paying of *zakah*[18] (obligatory poor-due) merely for the sake of fulfilling a requirement. It requires them to fulfill these obligations with utmost love and respect, as is mentioned in the following verses:

$$ لِّتُؤْمِنُواْ بِٱللَّهِ وَرَسُولِهِ وَتُعَزِّرُوهُ وَتُوَقِّرُوهُ $$

In order that you (O men) may believe in Allah and His Messenger, you may assist and honor Him. [Al-Fath, 48:9]

$$ فَٱلَّذِينَ ءَامَنُواْ بِهِ وَعَزَّرُوهُ $$

So it is those who believed in him and honored him. [Al-A'raf, 7:157]

That is why Allah commands believers to do everything that protects the honor and dignity of prophets and refrain from doing anything that may be disrespectful to them. The following verses of the Holy Quran allude to this subject:

---

[16] ركعة
[17] صلوة
[18] زكوة

يَـٰٓأَيُّهَا ٱلَّذِينَ ءَامَنُواْ لَا تَرْفَعُوٓاْ أَصْوَٰتَكُمْ فَوْقَ صَوْتِ ٱلنَّبِىِّ وَلَا تَجْهَرُواْ لَهُۥ بِٱلْقَوْلِ كَجَهْرِ بَعْضِكُمْ لِبَعْضٍ أَن تَحْبَطَ أَعْمَـٰلُكُمْ وَأَنتُمْ لَا تَشْعُرُونَ (2) إِنَّ ٱلَّذِينَ يَغُضُّونَ أَصْوَٰتَهُمْ عِندَ رَسُولِ ٱللَّهِ أُوْلَـٰٓئِكَ ٱلَّذِينَ ٱمْتَحَنَ ٱللَّهُ قُلُوبَهُمْ لِلتَّقْوَىٰ لَهُم مَّغْفِرَةٌ وَأَجْرٌ عَظِيمٌ (3)

O you who believe! Raise not your voices above the voice of the Prophet, nor speak aloud to him in talk, as you may speak aloud to one another, lest your deeds become vain and you perceive not. Those who lower their voices in the presence of Allah's Messenger, their hearts have been tested by Allah for piety; for them there is forgiveness and a great reward. [Al-Hujurat, 49:2-3]

لَّا تَجْعَلُواْ دُعَآءَ ٱلرَّسُولِ بَيْنَكُمْ كَدُعَآءِ بَعْضِكُم بَعْضًا

Make not the calling of the Messenger among you as your calling of one of another. [An-Nur, 24:63]

That is the very reason due to which it was forbidden for anyone to marry the wives of the Prophet (saw) after his death, as is mentioned in the following verse of the Holy Quran:

وَمَا كَانَ لَكُمْ أَن تُؤْذُواْ رَسُولَ ٱللَّهِ وَلَآ أَن تَنكِحُوٓاْ أَزْوَٰجَهُۥ مِنۢ بَعْدِهِۦٓ أَبَدًا إِنَّ ذَٰلِكُمْ كَانَ عِندَ ٱللَّهِ عَظِيمًا

And it is not for you to cause annoyance to the Messenger of Allah, nor that you should ever marry his wives after him; Lo! That in Allah's sight would be an enormity. [Al-Ahzab, 33:53]

In addition to the above verses of the Holy Quran, there are numerous *ahadith*[19] (sayings and practices of Prophet Muhammad) in which Muslims are commanded to love the Prophet (saw) more than anyone else. The following are a few examples in this regard:

The Prophet (saw) is reported to have said, "None of you shall become a true believer until I become dearer to you

---

[19] احاديث – plural of hadith

than your own son, father and all mankind.[20]" [*Sahih Bukhari, Kitabul Iman*]

The Prophet (saw) is reported to have said, "There are three things which, if acquired, will enable a person to taste the sweetness of *iman*; to love Allah and His Messenger more than anyone else; to love someone only for the sake of Allah; to abhor going back to *kufr* as much as one hates being thrown into fire." [*Sahih Bukhari, Kitabul Iman*]

It should be clearly understood that the relationship between prophets and the people whom they were sent to is not like the one that exists between a postman and the people to whom he delivers mail. The postman is only responsible for delivering the mail to the right recipient and he has nothing to do with the content of the mail or what the recipient does with it.

It is a mistake to consider that the relationship between prophets and the people whom they were sent to was only ceremonial and the prophets did not have much to do with the private, public and emotional life of people. It is in fact the result of not recognizing how lofty the position of prophets is. It is unfortunate that such an attitude has become common in this era, especially among those who are unaware of the position of *sunnah* (practices and sayings) of Prophet Muhammad (saw) and are influenced by the Christian and Western thinking.

The fact is that prophets are the best example for mankind to follow. They set the highest and most complete standard for human conduct and behavior. They are loved by Allah and their lifestyle, ways, habits and manners are dear to Him. Following their path is the easiest, shortest and surest way to gain nearness to Allah, as Allah Himself has ordered Prophet Muhammad (saw) to proclaim in the following verse of the Holy Quran:

$$\text{قُلْ إِن كُنتُمْ تُحِبُّونَ ٱللَّهَ فَٱتَّبِعُونِى يُحْبِبْكُمُ ٱللَّهُ وَيَغْفِرْ لَكُمْ ذُنُوبَكُمْ وَٱللَّهُ غَفُورٌ رَّحِيمٌ}$$

---

[20] In some narrations, it is also reported that he should love the Prophet more than even himself.

> Say, (O Muhammad, to mankind): If you love Allah,
> follow me; Allah will love you and forgive your sins.
> Allah is Forgiving, Merciful. [Al-Imran, 3:31]

On the other hand, liking and adopting the ways of those who are adamant in *kufr* and misguidance draws the anger and wrath of Allah, as is mentioned in the following verse of the Holy Quran:

$$\text{وَلَا تَرْكَنُواْ إِلَى ٱلَّذِينَ ظَلَمُواْ فَتَمَسَّكُمُ ٱلنَّارُ وَمَا لَكُم مِّن دُونِ ٱللَّهِ مِنْ أَوْلِيَآءَ ثُمَّ لَا تُنصَرُونَ}$$

> And incline not to those who do wrong, or the fire will
> seize you; and you have no protectors other than Allah,
> nor shall you be helped. [Hud, 11:113]

In the terminology of *Shari'ah*, the conduct of prophets is known as *Khasal Fitrah*[21] (ways of nature) and *Sunanul Huda*[22] (ways of guidance). This is what *Shari'ah* teaches and encourages. By imitating the ways and habits of prophets, one becomes their true replica, as the Holy Quran mentions:

$$\text{صِبْغَةَ ٱللَّهِ وَمَنْ أَحْسَنُ مِنَ ٱللَّهِ صِبْغَةً وَنَحْنُ لَهُ عَـٰبِدُونَ}$$

> We have taken the color of Allah and whose color is better
> than the color of Allah? Him alone we worship. [Al-
> Baqarah, 2:138]

This is the reason why *Shari'ah* differentiates between the ways of prophets and those of others. The ways of prophets are congruent with the laws of nature, whereas those of others are not. The ways of prophets are endowed with divine enlightenment and teachings whereas those of others are devoid of them. This distinction encompasses all aspects of human life including habits of eating (eating with the right hand instead of left), dressing (putting a garment first on the right side and then on the left side), and other chores of daily living.

It is thus incumbent upon us as the followers of Prophet Muhammad (saw) to go beyond the formal affiliation with him and his ways. We must

---

[21] خصل فطرة

[22] سنن الهدا

develop a deep emotional and passionate bond with the Prophet (saw) and his ways so that he and his ways become more beloved to us than our own lives, children, wealth and possessions, as is prescribed in the following a*hadith*:

> The Prophet (saw) is reported to have said, "None of you shall become a true believer until I become dearer to you than your own son, father and all the mankind." [*Sahih Bukhari, Kitabu Iman*]

> The Prophet (saw) is reported to have said, "A person cannot become a true *momin* (believer) until I become more beloved to him than his own person." [*Musnad Ahmad*[23]]

We also need to guard against the ways and forces which may weaken our bond with the Prophet (saw) and dampen our love and enthusiasm for his ways and lifestyle.

We need to constantly rejuvenate our attachment to the Prophet (saw) and his ways. A thoughtful study of the Quranic chapters such as Al-Ahzab (33), Al-Fath (48) and Al-Hujurat (49) goes a long way in providing necessary stimulus and boost in this respect.

Why do we have to recite *darood*[24] and *salawaat*[25] (salutation on prophets) in *tashahhud*[26] (sitting position in *salah* after two *rak'ah* and at the end) and funeral prayers? Why does the Holy Quran command us to send salutation to the Prophet (saw)? Why are there so many *ahadith* urging us to send *darood* and *salawaat* to the Prophet (saw)?

If we ponder over these questions, we can easily conclude that a believer is expected to have much more than just a formal attachment to the Prophet (saw) and he should not feel content with mere outward compliance of the laws of *Shari'ah*. A believer is actually expected to engender intense and overwhelming love and affection for the Prophet (saw) in his heart and mind. He is expected to have every fiber of his body filled with utmost love and devotion for the Prophet (saw). This is the kind of love and

---

[23] *Musnad Ahmad* is a collection of the sayings of Prophet Muhammad (saw).
[24] درود
[25] صلوات
[26] تشهد

reverence which the Holy Quran refers to by the words *taazeer*[27] and *tawqeer*[28] in the following verse:

$$\text{وَتُعَزِّرُوهُ وَتُوَقِّرُوهُ}$$

Assist and honor him [Al-Fath, 48:9]

This is the kind of love and devotion that was demonstrated by Khubaib bin 'Adi, Zaid bin Ad-Dathna[29], Abu Dujana[30], Talha bin 'Ubaidullah[31] and a woman[32] of the tribe of Bani Dinar for the Prophet (saw).

This is the kind of love, devotion and respect which had prompted 'Urwa bin Mas'ud Ath-Thaqafi[33] to say, "I have been to Chosroes, Caesar and Negus in their kingdoms, but have never seen any king being revered as Muhammad is revered by his Companions."

Similar was the remark of Abu Sufyan bin Harb who said, "I have never seen anyone loving someone as the Companions of Muhammad love him."

This is the kind of love with which *'ulama*, reformers and leaders, who had truly understood Islam and were chosen (by Allah) to serve and revive

---

[27] تعزير

[28] توقير

[29] When Zaid bin Ad-Dathna was being taken to the site of execution after the incident of Ar-Raji, Abu Sufyan asked him,"Don't you wish that Muhammad had been here in your place and you be with your family?" "By God," replied Zaid, "I don't wish Muhammad to be hurt even by a thorn in the place where he is and I am sitting in the comfort of my home." Thereupon Abu Sufyan remarked, "I have never seen any man adored as Muhammad is adored by his companions." Zaid was killed thereafter. [Seerah Ibn Hisham, vol. II, page 172]

[30] Abu Dujana stood in front of the Prophet in the battle of Uhad and shielded him by taking the arrows at his back.

[31] Talha bin 'Ubaidullah shielded the Prophet (saw) in the battle of Uhad with his hands against the arrows due to which his hands became incapacitated

[32] A lady belonging to the tribe of Bani Dinar had lost her husband, father, and brother in the battle of Uhad. When she was informed about it, she said, "Tell me how is the Messenger of Allah?" The people told her that the Messenger of Allah was alright. She said, "Let me have a glimpse of him." When she saw the Messenger of Allah, she said, "No calamity means anything as long as you are here."

[33] 'Urwa bin Mas'ud Ath-Thaqafi had come on behalf of the Quraish of Makkah to the Messenger of Allah to negotiate the Treaty of Hudaibiyah.

Islam, were blessed in abundance. This love is so powerful that it can cure spiritual diseases, beautify human character and infuse a new breath of life in a person as does the morning breeze to flowers. However, it must be within the boundaries of *Shari'ah* and on the pattern of the Companions of the Prophet (saw).

Without this kind of love, it is not possible to remain steadfast on the *sunnah* of the Prophet (saw) and orders of *Shari'ah* in all circumstances. When Muslims possessed the true love of Allah and His Prophet, they were shining like a bright star. Without that love, they have now become a heap of cold burnt ash.

Real Accomplishment of Prophets

Modern society and its institutions have utterly failed in producing people who are capable of steering humanity in the right direction. They can harness solar energy, build vehicles which can travel in space reaching distant planets, and produce and control atomic energy. They can alleviate poverty and shortage of food, make an entire nation literate and excel in science and technology. There is no doubt that these achievements are astonishing and mind-boggling. Yet, the utter impotence of modern society in producing and nurturing men who possess correct belief and high moral character is its greatest failure and misfortune.

People have started losing confidence in scientific and industrial advancements. It is feared that in reaction to modern materialistic advancements and progress, a revolt may be brewing which modern society will not be able to withstand. If termites have eaten every plank, it is unrealistic to think that such planks may be used to build a ship that can weather a fierce storm. In the same way, if individuals have become corrupt, dishonest and immoral, it is unrealistic to expect that they can become the foundation of a sound, healthy and just society.

Individuals who are the product of a materialistic society are generally devoid of *iman* and human conscience; are less concerned about others' feelings and needs; and lack compassion and love for humanity. They are more likely to be self-centered and devoted to the fulfillment of their own desires and needs. Their scope of concern may extend at most to their own community or country (and not to the entire mankind). Such people cannot be expected to build and establish a god-fearing, pious and tranquil society whether they call themselves democrats, capitalists, socialists or communists. They cannot be trusted as the shepherds of humanity.

It is only the rank of prophets which has been able to produce best individuals and establish an ideal society. They were able to transform the hearts and minds of people. Under their stewardship, people were able to subdue their ego, develop liking for virtuous deeds and aversion for evil deeds and dispel the delusion of wealth and power.

Prophets did not teach science to mankind. They did not bring new discoveries and inventions to the world. It was not an act of negligence and they did not need to apologize for it. They in fact gave to the world something which was much more important than science, inventions and discoveries. They nurtured people who could keep themselves on the right path and also lead humanity in that direction. Such people know who their Creator is, what the purpose of their life is, how to benefit from things around them, how to benefit and serve others, how to draw favors of Allah and how to utilize the wealth and power which Allah has given to them. Such people are a blessing for the world and they represent the real accomplishment of prophets.

Finality of Prophethood – A Logical Necessity

Divine religion has been perfected with the coming of Prophet Muhammad (saw). Prophet Muhammad (saw) is the final Messenger of Allah. Islam is the final message and complete way of life. These are among the core beliefs of the *ummah*[34] (followers) of Prophet Muhammad (saw).

A Jewish scholar (Tariq bin Shihab) expressed his envy and surprise to 'Umar (ra) by saying, "You recite a verse[35] which, if it had been revealed in relation to us, we would have taken that day as the day of rejoicing." Thereupon 'Umar (ra) said, "I know where it was revealed, which day it was revealed and where the Allah's Messenger was at the time it was revealed. It was revealed on the day of 'Arafah (ninth day of Dhul Hijjah), it was Friday and we were in 'Arafat with Allah's Messenger." [*Sahih Muslim, Kitab Al-Tafsir*]

The belief that Prophet Muhammad (saw) is the final Messenger and the religion of Islam has reached perfection has saved the *ummah* from being shattered into pieces by many fake claimants (of prophethood) who have appeared from time to time in the last fourteen centuries. This pillar of

---

[34] امة

[35] "This day I have perfected for you your religion and completed My favor upon you and have approved for you Islam as your religion" [Al-Maidah, 5:3].

faith (i.e. Prophet Muhammad is the final prophet and Islam has reached the state of perfection and completion) has proven extremely powerful in deflecting all kinds of attacks, conspiracies, distortions and distractions and in keeping the *ummah* intact. If it was not for this pillar of faith, this *ummah* would have met the same fate as its predecessors. It would have splintered into many factions and each faction would have its own book, history, spiritual leadership and culture.

The fact that the prophethood has terminated is a matter of great honor and blessing for mankind. It is a declaration that mankind has reached the age of adulthood and has matured to accept the final message of Allah. It now does not need a new revelation, a new message and a new way of life. It gives man more confidence since he knows that the divine religion has reached its highest point.

Man now does not need to look behind. He does not need to look at the heavens to get new revelation. He just needs to work hard to benefit from the unlimited treasures of Allah using the principles of Islam and *Shari'ah* which have been perfected and completed with the coming of Prophet Muhammad (saw). Had not the prophethood reached its finality, man would have always remained shaky, uncertain and unsatisfied about his future.

Coming of Prophet Muhammad (saw)

In the 6th century after Prophet Isa (*alaihis salaam*), the world was on the brink of committing suicide and it appeared that the entire mankind was briskly preparing for it. No artist, writer or historian could render a better picture of it than how the Holy Quran has described it in the following verse:

وَٱذْكُرُوا نِعْمَتَ ٱللَّهِ عَلَيْكُمْ إِذْ كُنتُمْ أَعْدَاءً فَأَلَّفَ بَيْنَ قُلُوبِكُمْ فَأَصْبَحْتُم بِنِعْمَتِهِ إِخْوَانًا وَكُنتُمْ عَلَىٰ شَفَا حُفْرَةٍ مِّنَ ٱلنَّارِ فَأَنقَذَكُم مِّنْهَا

Remember with gratitude Allah's favor on you; for you were enemies and He joined your hearts in love, so that by His Grace, you became brethren; and you were on the brink of the pit of fire, and He saved you from it. [Al-Imran, 3:103]

It is beyond the capacity of present-day historians and writers to portray the condition that was prevailing in the world at that time. There are no words which can fully express the severity of vice, chaos and disorder which was gripping mankind. It is not possible to fathom the depth of ignorance and darkness into which humanity had fallen.

Moral decay was not only confined to a few tribes or nations. Drinking, gambling, prostitution, oppression, injustice and crime were rampant. Idol worshipping was the order of the day. The world was ruled by tyrant kings and oppressive regimes.

It is true that some stone-hearted Arabs were burying their daughters alive with their own hands because they felt ashamed of being the father of a female child. But the reality is that the entire mankind was poised to bury and annihilate itself.

Since that period is now far behind us, it is impossible to visualize it and draw a true picture of it. Only those who had lived through those times could have accurately portrayed it.

Just to get an idea of how dreadful the condition was, let us imagine that mankind is standing in the shape of an extremely handsome person. He is the one upon whom the continuity of the human race is dependent. He is the one in front of whom the angels were asked to prostrate. He is the one whom Allah made His *khalifah*[36] (vicegerent) on the face of the earth. He is the one for whom the entire universe was created and decorated. He is the one due to whom this universe is alive and bustling. Now imagine that he is standing in front of an ocean of fire which is limitless in length, width and depth and he is only moments away from plunging into it to disappear forever. This is probably the best portrayal of the condition that was prevailing when Prophet Muhammad (saw) came to this world, as the Holy Quran has mentioned:

$$\text{وَكُنتُمْ عَلَىٰ شَفَا حُفْرَةٍ مِّنَ ٱلنَّارِ فَأَنقَذَكُم مِّنْهَا}$$

> You were on the brink of the pit of fire, and He saved you
> from it. [Al-Imran, 3:103]

The same has been described by the Prophet (saw) in the following *hadith*:

---

[36] خليفة

> Narrated Abu Hurairah: I heard Allah's Messenger saying,
> "My example and the example of the people is like that of
> a man who lit a fire and when its light spread all over,
> moths and insects started falling into it. The man tried to
> prevent them (from falling in the fire) but they did not
> listen to him and fell into the fire. Likewise I am holding
> you by your waist and warning you not to fall into the fire
> (of Hell), but you insist on falling into it." [*Sahih Bukhari,
> Kitabur Riqaq*]

Before the coming of Prophet Muhammad (saw), ignorance and immorality had debauched the society to such an extent that a man, instead of feeling empathy for the pain and suffering of another man, used to take pleasure and enjoyment in witnessing it. The history of the Roman Empire, which is known for its might and grandeur, bears ample testimony to it. Hartpole Lecky wrote in his book *History of European Morals from Augustus to Charlemagne* that the most enjoyable and thrilling moment for the Romans, who were watching a gladiator game, was when a gladiator was going through the last pangs of his death while defending himself against a beastly animal; the spectators would become so excited and rowdy that police had to intervene to calm them down. In that game, humans were placed in an enclosure and forced to defend themselves against extremely fierce animals; this game was very popular among the elites of the Roman society. Lecky writes:

> Nor was this fascination surprising, for no pageant has
> ever combined more powerful elements of attraction. The
> magnificent Circus, the gorgeous dresses of the assembled
> Court, the contagion of a passionate enthusiasm thrilling
> almost visibly through the mighty throng, the breathless
> silence of expectation, the wild cheers bursting
> simultaneously from eighty thousand tongues, and
> echoing to the farthest outskirts of the city, the rapid
> alternations of the fray, the deeds of splendid courage that
> were manifested, were all well fitted to entrance the
> imagination. [Page 286, Vol. 1]

Thus the main problem was that humanity had lost all of its noble instincts and degraded itself into a species of wild animals. In other words, it had become totally inhuman and had turned itself in the court of Allah to be dealt with the severest punishment. That is when Allah sent His Messenger

Prophet Muhammad (saw) to this world, as Allah has mentioned in the Holy Quran:

$$\text{وَمَآ أَرْسَلْنَاكَ إِلَّا رَحْمَةً لِّلْعَالَمِينَ}$$

We sent you not, but as a Mercy for all creatures. [Al-Anbiya, 21:107]

Prophet Muhammad (saw) came as the prophet for the entire mankind and for the entire period until the Last Day. The very first thing that he did was to remove the sword which was hanging at the head of humanity ready to strike a fatal blow at any moment. He gave to humanity a new lease on life. He revived its honor, dignity and mission. He enabled it to embark upon a new era in human history. He set it on the path of building a new civilization and culture. He led it to conquer new heights of enlightenment and spirituality. In fact, he brought an entirely new world into existence.

Allah's Favors to Mankind through Prophet Muhammad (saw)

The favors that Allah bestowed upon mankind through Prophet Muhammad (saw) are innumerable; the following is only a short list of the same.

1. Tawheed
2. Universal Brotherhood
3. Recognition of man as the best creation
4. Revival of hope in the mercy of Allah
5. Harmony between *deen* and *dunya*
6. Correct understanding of success

1. *Tawheed*

The greatest gift that Prophet Muhammad (saw) gave to mankind was the reintroduction of the *'aqeedah* of *Tawheed* which had been almost completely forgotten and abandoned. He presented this *'aqeedah* in such a dynamic way that it revolutionized the entire world.

Man had excelled in poetry, philosophy and politics. He had ruled nations and countries. He had overpowered the four basic elements of nature — fire, wind, water and soil. He had made flowers blossom out of rock. He had torn apart mountains to make room for rivers to flow. He had even raised himself to the status of god. Yet he had bowed his head in front of creatures which were lifeless and much weaker than him. He had kneeled before things which he had created with his own hands. He had worshipped things such as mountains, rivers, trees, ghosts, insects and animals. He had feared these objects and supplicated to them for his needs. The result was that he had become cowardly, superstitious and disoriented.

Prophet Muhammad (saw) gave man a straightforward, simple, pure and dynamic faith which enabled him to recognize the real creator and gain complete freedom from everything else. Man gained new strength, new vigor, new courage and a new mission for life. Man became firm in his belief that Allah is the only doer of everything and that He is the only One who can harm or benefit anyone. Man's life changed; his thinking changed; he freed himself from all kinds of slavery; he became fearless; he gained confidence and became firm. Man started believing that he is subservient to Allah only and Allah has made him superior to all other creations. The result was that man once again understood and recognized his position as the best creation of Allah.

After the coming of Prophet Muhammad (saw), the impact of the message of *Tawheed* started having its effect on all other philosophies and religions. The religions which were the staunchest proponents of *shirk* felt compelled to declare in one form or the other that there is only one god. They felt compelled to camouflage their polytheistic beliefs so that they could avoid being branded as polytheists and their belief system would look somewhat similar to that of *Tawheed*. They started feeling ashamed of their polytheistic beliefs and practices. They started losing confidence in their polytheistic beliefs and felt inferior to the belief system of *Tawheed*.

2. Universal Brotherhood

The second most precious gift that Prophet Muhammad (saw) gave to mankind was the concept of universal brotherhood. People were divided into tribes, castes and classes. The concept of master and slave, lord and subject, and upper and lower caste was pervasive in the society. The concept of equality was nonexistent. After centuries, Prophet Muhammad (saw) made the following historical declaration:

> People! You all have one Creator. You all come from the same father, Adam. You all are made of clay. In the eyesight of Allah, the most elevated is the one who is most

pious. No Arab is superior to a non-Arab except on the basis of piety.

The Prophet (saw) made this declaration during his last *hajj* (632 AD) in the presence of a huge gathering of about 124,000 followers. The declaration included two fundamental principles:

1. All humans have been created by the same Creator (Allah).
2. All humans are children of the same father (Adam).

Thus every person is related to all other persons in two ways: spiritually (because of having the same Creator) and physically (because of having the same father). These principles served as the foundation of a society in which the entire humanity could prosper and find peace.

At the time this declaration was made, mankind was not ready for such a revolutionary concept and thus it was felt as an earthquake and a bolt of lightning. However, due to the pioneering efforts of the Islamic states, jurists, scholars and reformers and the advancements which mankind has made in past centuries, what was once unthinkable has now become commonplace. For example, the United Nations adopted the Universal Declaration of Human Rights (UDHR) in 1948 and every country and institution of the world now makes it an integral part of its constitution.

At the time Prophet Muhammad (saw) made this declaration, it was believed that people of a certain creed and denomination were superior to others by birth and that they were directly related to god, the sun or the moon, as the Holy Quran mentions about the Jews and Christians:

وَقَالَتِ ٱلْيَهُودُ وَٱلنَّصَـٰرَىٰ نَحْنُ أَبْنَـٰٓؤُا۟ ٱللَّهِ وَأَحِبَّـٰٓؤُهُ

> The Jews and Christians say: "We are sons of Allah and are His beloved." [Al-Maidah, 5:18]

The Pharaohs of Egypt used to consider themselves as representatives of the sun whom they worshipped as god. The Rajputs of India still believe that their origin is either solar (*suraj bansi*) or lunar (*chandra bansi*). The Chosroes (kings of the Sassanian dynasty of Iran) used to believe that they were related to god by blood and that they were by birth superior to others; the last king of the Sassanian dynasty was named Yazdagird which meant that he was very close and dear to god. The Chinese used to consider their kings the sons of the sky; they used to believe that the sky was a male, the earth was a female, the universe was the product of the two and the king was their first son.

Arabs used to consider non-Arabs dumb and inarticulate. The Quraish used to consider themselves as the best and most sacred among all the Arabs. That is why they had reserved for themselves the most exalted and prestigious duties during the *hajj* period. That was the context in which the Holy Quran made the following declaration:

$$يَـٰٓأَيُّهَا ٱلنَّاسُ إِنَّا خَلَقۡنَـٰكُم مِّن ذَكَرٍ وَأُنثَىٰ وَجَعَلۡنَـٰكُمۡ شُعُوبٗا وَقَبَآئِلَ لِتَعَارَفُوٓاْ إِنَّ أَكۡرَمَكُمۡ عِندَ ٱللَّهِ أَتۡقَىٰكُمۡ إِنَّ ٱللَّهَ عَلِيمٌ خَبِيرٌ$$

O mankind! We created you from a single (pair) of a male and a female, and made you into nations and tribes, that you may know each other (not that you may despise each other); Verily the most honored of you in the sight of Allah is (he who is) the most righteous of you; And Allah has full knowledge and is well acquainted (with all things). [Al-Hujurat, 49:13]

No person is superior to others except due to his piety. No one except Allah is praiseworthy, as the Holy Quran states in its very first and most widely recited chapter Al-Fatiha:

$$ٱلۡحَمۡدُ لِلَّهِ رَبِّ ٱلۡعَـٰلَمِينَ$$

All praise is due to Allah, the Lord of all the worlds. [Al-Fatihah, 1:1]

3. Recognition of Man's Status as the Best Creation

The third most precious gift that Prophet Muhammad (saw) gave to mankind was the concept that man is superior to every creation of this universe. At the time the Prophet (saw) came to this world, man had no value and many animals, trees and other such objects were considered more sacred and valuable than human beings; human blood and flesh were sacrificed for the sake of these objects.

Prophet Muhammad (saw) presented the concept that man is the best creation of Allah, he (man) is the *khalifah* of Allah on the earth and all other creations of the universe have been created to serve him (man), as the Holy Quran has mentioned:

$$\text{هُوَ ٱلَّذِى خَلَقَ لَكُم مَّا فِى ٱلْأَرْضِ جَمِيعًا}$$

It is He who created for you all of that which is on the earth. [Al-Baqarah, 2:29]

$$\text{وَلَقَدْ كَرَّمْنَا بَنِىٓ ءَادَمَ وَحَمَلْنَـٰهُمْ فِى ٱلْبَرِّ وَٱلْبَحْرِ وَرَزَقْنَـٰهُم مِّنَ ٱلطَّيِّبَـٰتِ وَفَضَّلْنَـٰهُمْ عَلَىٰ كَثِيرٍ مِّمَّنْ خَلَقْنَا تَفْضِيلاً}$$

We have honored the sons of Adam, provided them with transport on land and sea, given them for sustenance things good and pure, and conferred on them special favors, above a great part of our creation. [Al-Isra, 17:70]

The following *ahadith* further solidify man's position by emphasizing how dear he is to Allah and how close a person may get to Allah by being kind and merciful to his fellow human beings.

All creatures are Allah's family (dependents) and Allah loves most those who treat His dependents well and kindly [*Baihaqi*[37]].

Abu Huraira reported Allah's Messenger as saying: Verily, Allah, the Exalted, would say on the Day of Judgment: O son of Adam! I was sick but you did not visit Me. He would say: O my Lord! How could I visit You as You are the Lord of the worlds? Thereupon Allah would say: Didn't you know that such and such servant of Mine was sick but you did not visit him and were you not aware that if you had visited him, you would have found Me by him? O son of Adam! I asked food from you but you did not feed Me. He would say: My Lord! How could I feed You as You are the Lord of the worlds? Allah would say: Didn't you know that such and such servant of Mine asked food from you but you did not feed him, and were you not aware that if you had fed him, you would have found Me by his side? Allah would again say: O son of Adam! I

---

[37] *Baihaqi* is a collection of the sayings of Prophet Muhammad (saw).

> asked drink from you but you did not provide Me drink. He would say: My Lord! How could I provide You drink as You are the Lord of the worlds? Thereupon Allah would say: Such and such servant of Mine asked you for a drink but you did not provide him and had you provided him drink, you would have found Me near him. [*Sahih Muslim, Kitab Al-Birr was-Salat-I-wal-Adab*]

Can there be any declaration more forceful than this regarding the status of human being? Does any other religion or philosophy give such an elevated position to man? Prophet Muhammad (saw) declared, as reported in the following *hadith*, that the most powerful means of drawing Allah's mercy is to show mercy to His creations.

> The mercy of the Compassionate Almighty Allah descends upon those who are merciful. If you show mercy to the dwellers of the earth, He Who is in the heavens will show mercy to you. [*Sunan Abu Dawud*[38], *Kitab Al-Adab*]

Just imagine how dreadful a society would be when a man considered his fellow human beings as subhuman. Thousands of lives used to be squandered for the pleasure of a single individual. There were rulers who devastated country after country. Alexander (356-323 BC) came from Macedonia up to India and demolished many nations and civilizations on the way. Julius Caesarr (100-44 BC) killed people savagely. More recently, millions of people lost their lives in the two world wars of the 20th century. All of this happened due to ego, arrogance, greed for power and control of the economy.

4. Revival of Hope in the Mercy of Allah

The fourth most precious gift that Prophet Muhammad (saw) gave to mankind was the restoration of its confidence in its ability and potential. It enabled man to once again set out on the journey of scaling new heights of success and achievement.

At the time Prophet Muhammad (saw) came to this world, humanity was suffering from despair and hopelessness and had lost hope in the mercy of Allah. The dogmatic beliefs of the ancient religions of Asia and the

---

[38] *Sunan Abu Dawud* is a collection of the sayings of Prophet Muhammad (saw).

distorted doctrines of Christianity (which was prevalent in the Middle East and Europe) had played a major role in precipitating that thinking.

In Hinduism and other ancient religions of India, the concept of transmigration (*Ava-gavan*) leaves no choice in the hands of a man, as he must continue perpetually in the cycle of births and deaths, suffering and sinning in the process. In Christianity, according to the doctrine of "original sin," all humans are born with a predisposition to sinful behavior and Prophet Isa (*alaihis salaam*) died for the sins of human beings. Such beliefs had thrown large populations of the world into a state of despair about their future and they had lost hope in the mercy of God.

Prophet Muhammad (saw) clearly declared that a man's *fitrah*[39] (nature, disposition) is like a clean slate with nothing written on it from before and that man is capable of inscribing the best writing on it. A man makes or breaks this life and the Hereafter by his deeds. No one is responsible for the deeds of others. The Holy Quran has repeatedly mentioned that no one will carry the burden of any other person in the Hereafter, but everyone will face the consequences of his own deeds only and everyone will be fully rewarded for all of his deeds.

$$\text{أَلَّا تَزِرُ وَازِرَةٌ وِزْرَ أُخْرَىٰ (38) وَأَن لَّيْسَ لِلْإِنسَٰنِ إِلَّا مَا}$$
$$\text{سَعَىٰ (39) وَأَنَّ سَعْيَهُ سَوْفَ يُرَىٰ (40) ثُمَّ يُجْزَىٰهُ ٱلْجَزَآءَ}$$
$$\text{ٱلْأَوْفَىٰ (41)}$$

No bearer of burdens will bear the burden of another. That man can have nothing but what he strives for. That (the fruit of) his striving will soon come in sight. Then he will be rewarded with a reward complete. [An-Najm, 53:38-41]

Prophet Muhammad (saw) declared that the state of indulgence in wrongdoing or transgression is a temporary one in which a person falls due to his ignorance or provocation of Satan. Man's innate quality is that he leans towards what is righteous and feels sorry for his mistakes. He has inherited from Prophet Adam (*alaihis salaam*) the desire to confess his wrong, repent for his sins, cry before Allah, seek His forgiveness and vow not to wrong again.

---

[39] فطرة

The world had lost hope in the divine mercy and had believed that it could never come out of the curse of its sins. But the Prophet (saw) opened the door of repentance and revived the practice of repentance once again. He propagated it so passionately that one of his names is *Nabi-ut-taubah*[40] (The Prophet of Repentance).

The Prophet (saw) did not present repentance as a despicable and reprehensible act. He instead described it as an act of worship, an act that is very dear to Allah and an act that can be a means of gaining nearness to Allah. He elevated this act to such an extent that people who were innocent and did not commit wrong envied those who wronged and repented.

The Holy Quran has beautifully described the effect of repentance in earning forgiveness and wiping out sins. It passionately invites those who have fallen victim to Satan and vain desires to take advantage of the infinite mercy of Allah. It describes the compassion and benevolence of Allah in such a way that Allah appears to be more eager to forgive sinners than sinners are to seek His forgiveness, as is evident from the following verse of the Holy Quran:

قُلْ يَـٰعِبَادِىَ ٱلَّذِينَ أَسْرَفُواْ عَلَىٰٓ أَنفُسِهِمْ لَا تَقْنَطُواْ مِن رَّحْمَةِ ٱللَّهِ إِنَّ ٱللَّهَ يَغْفِرُ ٱلذُّنُوبَ جَمِيعًا إِنَّهُۥ هُوَ ٱلْغَفُورُ ٱلرَّحِيمُ

Say: "O my Servants who have transgressed against their souls! Despair not of the Mercy of Allah; for Allah forgives all sins; for He is Oft-Forgiving, Most Merciful. [Az-Zumar, 39:53]

In another verse, Allah mentions the sinners and wrongdoers among the dwellers of Paradise:

وَسَارِعُوٓاْ إِلَىٰ مَغْفِرَةٍ مِّن رَّبِّكُمْ وَجَنَّةٍ عَرْضُهَا ٱلسَّمَـٰوَٰتُ وَٱلْأَرْضُ أُعِدَّتْ لِلْمُتَّقِينَ (133) ٱلَّذِينَ يُنفِقُونَ فِى ٱلسَّرَّآءِ وَٱلضَّرَّآءِ وَٱلْكَـٰظِمِينَ ٱلْغَيْظَ وَٱلْعَافِينَ عَنِ ٱلنَّاسِ وَٱللَّهُ يُحِبُّ ٱلْمُحْسِنِينَ (134) وَٱلَّذِينَ إِذَا فَعَلُواْ فَـٰحِشَةً أَوْ ظَلَمُوٓاْ أَنفُسَهُمْ ذَكَرُواْ ٱللَّهَ فَٱسْتَغْفَرُواْ لِذُنُوبِهِمْ وَمَن يَغْفِرُ ٱلذُّنُوبَ إِلَّا ٱللَّهُ وَلَمْ يُصِرُّواْ عَلَىٰ مَا فَعَلُواْ وَهُمْ يَعْلَمُونَ (135) أُوْلَـٰٓئِكَ جَزَآؤُهُم

نبي التوبة ⁴⁰

مَّغْفِرَةٌ مِّن رَّبِّهِمْ وَجَنَّـٰتٌ تَجْرِى مِن تَحْتِهَا ٱلْأَنْهَـٰرُ خَـٰلِدِينَ فِيهَاۚ

وَنِعْمَ أَجْرُ ٱلْعَـٰمِلِينَ (136)

Be quick in the race for forgiveness from your Lord, and
for a Garden whose width is that (of the whole) of the
heavens and of the earth, prepared for the righteous. Those
who spend (freely), whether in prosperity or in adversity,
who restrain anger, and pardon (all) men; Allah loves
those who do good deeds. And those who, having done
something to be ashamed of, or wronged their own souls,
earnestly bring Allah to mind, and ask for forgiveness for
their sins; and who can forgive sins except Allah? And are
never obstinate in persisting knowingly in (the wrong)
they have done. For such, the reward is forgiveness from
their Lord and gardens with rivers flowing underneath, an
eternal dwelling; how excellent a recompense for those
who work (and strive)! [Al-Imran, 3:133-136]

The position of those who repent is so elevated that the Holy Quran has
mentioned them even before the worshipping and pious people in the
following verse while enumerating those who are deemed *momineen*[41]
(believers):

ٱلتَّـٰئِبُونَ ٱلْعَـٰبِدُونَ ٱلْحَـٰمِدُونَ ٱلسَّـٰئِحُونَ ٱلرَّٰكِعُونَ ٱلسَّـٰجِدُونَ

ٱلْآمِرُونَ بِٱلْمَعْرُوفِ وَٱلنَّاهُونَ عَنِ ٱلْمُنكَرِ وَٱلْحَـٰفِظُونَ

لِحُدُودِ ٱللَّهِۗ وَبَشِّرِ ٱلْمُؤْمِنِينَ

Those who turn (to Allah) in repentance, those who
worship Him, those who praise Him, those who strive in
the way of Allah, those who bow down in *ruku*, those who
prostrate in *sajdah*, those who enjoin good and forbid evil
and those who observe the limit set by Allah. Proclaim the
glad tidings to the believers. [At-Taubah, 9:112]

A glowing testimony to the status of those who repent appears in the
Quranic verse which was revealed to declare the acceptance of repentance
of the three Companions (Ka'b bin Malik, Murara bin Ar-Rabi'and Hilal
bin Omaiyah) who had failed to join the Prophet (saw) in the expedition of
Tabuk (9th Hijri) without any legitimate excuse:

---

[41] مومنين

لَّقَد تَّابَ اللَّهُ عَلَى النَّبِىِّ وَالْمُهَـٰجِرِينَ وَالْأَنصَارِ الَّذِينَ اتَّبَعُوهُ فِى سَاعَةِ الْعُسْرَةِ مِن بَعْدِ مَا كَادَ يَزِيغُ قُلُوبُ فَرِيقٍ مِّنْهُمْ ثُمَّ تَابَ عَلَيْهِمْ إِنَّهُ بِهِمْ رَءُوفٌ رَّحِيمٌ (117) وَعَلَى الثَّلَـٰثَةِ الَّذِينَ خُلِّفُوا حَتَّىٰ إِذَا ضَاقَتْ عَلَيْهِمُ الْأَرْضُ بِمَا رَحُبَتْ وَضَاقَتْ عَلَيْهِمْ أَنفُسُهُمْ وَظَنُّوا أَن لَّا مَلْجَأَ مِنَ اللَّهِ إِلَّا إِلَيْهِ ثُمَّ تَابَ عَلَيْهِمْ لِيَتُوبُوا إِنَّ اللَّهَ هُوَ التَّوَّابُ الرَّحِيمُ (118)

Surely, Allah has favored the Prophet and the Emigrants (*Muhajirin*) and the Supporters (*Ansar*) who followed him in the hour of hardship after the hearts of a group of them had nearly swerved. Surely, He is very kind and merciful to them. And He also favored those three whose matter was deferred until the earth became straitened for them despite all of its vastness, and even their own souls had become straitened for them, and they realized that there is no refuge from Allah, except in Him. He then turned towards them so that they may repent. Surely, Allah is the most Relenting, the most Merciful. [At-Taubah, 9:117-118]

There is a very fine point for why the Holy Quran chose to mention (in the above verse) the Prophet (saw) and other Companions (who had joined him in the expedition of Tabuk) before mentioning the three who had remained behind. It has done so to make sure that those three Companions do not feel slighted, they remain free from any blemish in the eyesight of others and it becomes clear to the reciters of the Holy Quran forever that those three (despite missing the Tabuk expedition) did in fact belong to the front row of the truthful Companions. What could be a better way of complimenting those who repent?

Allah has also declared that His mercy prevails over His anger and might:

وَرَحْمَتِى وَسِعَتْ كُلَّ شَىْءٍ

My mercy encompasses all things. [Al-A'raf, 7:156]

It comes in a *hadith Qudsi*[42] that Allah says, "My mercy prevails over My anger.'

Allah has termed despair as *kufr*, ignorance and misguidance as Prophet Yaqoob (*alaihis salaam*) declared in the following verse:

$$\text{إِنَّهُ لَا يَأْيَسُ مِن رَّوْحِ ٱللَّهِ إِلَّا ٱلْقَوْمُ ٱلْكَٰفِرُونَ}$$

> Truly no one despairs of Allah's Mercy, except those who
> have no faith. [Yusuf, 12:87]

Prophet Ibrahim (*alaihis salaam*) declared as follows:

$$\text{وَمَن يَقْنَطُ مِن رَّحْمَةِ رَبِّهِ إِلَّا ٱلضَّآلُّونَ}$$

> And who despairs of the mercy of his Lord except those
> who have gone astray? [Al-Hijr, 15:56]

Prophet Muhammad (saw), by relating the virtues of repentance and the mercy of Allah, gave a new message of hope, removed the despair and fear which had been instilled in the minds of people (by Jewish scholars, interpreters of the old scriptures and Christian advocates of monasticism). He gave to humanity a fresh breath of life, revived its self-confidence and elevated it from the position of disgrace to that of honor and dignity.

5. Harmony between *Deen* and *Dunya*

The fifth most precious gift that Prophet Muhammad (saw) gave to mankind is the understanding that there is no conflict between *deen* (religion, Life Hereafter) and *dunya* (this life, worldly pursuit) and both go hand in hand.

The outcome and effect of one's deeds and actions depend upon the person's intent and purpose which is known as *niyah*[43] (intention) in the Islamic terminology. It is a simple term, but has a very comprehensive and deep meaning.

---

[42] Hadith Qudsi is a sub-category of hadith. These are in fact the words of Allah which Prophet Muhammad has communicated in his own words.

[43] نية

Any act, be it related to war, earning of livelihood, fulfillment of personal, family and social needs, acquirement of worldly possessions and indulgence in permitted forms of travel and tourism, etc., if done for the pleasure of Allah is pure *deen* and can be a means of gaining nearness to Allah. On the other hand, any act of worship, devotion and holiness which is devoid of the intention of pleasing Allah and gaining reward from Him is pure *dunya* and will not fetch any reward.

Past religions had divided life into two disjoint compartments - *deen* and *dunya* - and people were divided into two camps: those who pursued the path of *deen* and those who pursued the path of *dunya*. There was a huge wall dividing the two camps and each camp harbored deep rivalry, enmity and hostility towards the other. It was not possible for a person to remain associated with both the camps simultaneously, and it was imperative that a person of one camp be at war with the other camp.

It had become a common belief that it was impossible for a person to be religious unless he completely disassociated himself from all worldly pursuits, shirked all worldly responsibilities, shunned all human desires and abandoned all types of comfort, power and position. Since man by nature loves ease, comfort and pleasure, a religion in which there is no provision for man to indulge in permitted forms of fun, pleasure and comfort becomes unacceptable and unbearable to most people. That is the reason why most people chose *dunya* over *deen* and became fully immersed in *dunya* by abandoning *deen*.

This is the main reason why political and governmental institutions revolted against the church in Europe and freed themselves from religious constraints. As a result of that separation, society turned into an elephant without chains and a camel without reins.

The estrangement between *deen* and *dunya* not only deprived mankind of the benefits of a noble and righteous society, but it also opened the door of hostility and antagonism towards religion among common people. Europe became the first victim of this calamity followed by many other nations and countries. Today, as a result of the wall of separation that has been erected between *deen* and *dunya*, the world has reached the lowest point of immorality and disgrace.

Thus one of the greatest gifts of Prophet Muhammad (saw) to mankind was that he integrated *deen* and *dunya* together and dispelled the misconception of *deen* versus *dunya*. He transformed the entire human life into an act of worship and the entire earth into a place of worship. He joined people from warring camps into a single arena where everyone strives to do good deeds, serve mankind and seek the pleasure of Allah. In that arena, it will not be hard to find a pious person dressed in worldly attire, an ascetic in the form of a king, a daytime warrior crying in front of Allah in the night and a swordsman busy in the remembrance of Allah.

6. Correct Understanding of Success

The sixth most precious gift that Prophet Muhammad (saw) gave to mankind is the true understanding of success and the final destination.

Mankind had forgotten its ultimate objective, its final destination and how best its talents and capabilities may be utilized. Different people had different understanding of success and everyone was striving day and night to achieve that according to his own understanding. Some believed that it was in accumulating huge amounts of wealth; some believed that it was in acquiring power, authority and dominance over land; some believed that it was in the fulfillment of desires; some believed that it was in imitating certain individuals; and some believed that it was in acquiring skills in poetry and literature.

Prophet Muhammad (saw) presented the true picture of success to the world. He instilled in the minds of people that the real objective is to recognize the real Creator, know His power and attributes and develop true love for Him. He taught them that real success lies in developing firm *iman* and *yaqeen* and in acquiring inner qualities. He taught them that they could earn the pleasure of Allah by serving fellow human beings and sacrificing their own needs for others. He showed that these are the real avenues of success and man could surpass even the angels in piety and spirituality.

The coming of Prophet Muhammad (saw) changed the temperament of the world. People changed and their hearts overflowed with the love of Allah. They charged themselves with the mission of pleasing Allah, connecting every single soul to the Creator and benefiting others.

When the rainy season begins and rain water starts pouring, greenery comes to life everywhere, dry branches and leaves start turning green and new buds of flower start sprouting. Similar was the case when Prophet Muhammad (saw) came to this world. Millions of people changed the direction of their lives. They set out to achieve their new goal with unlimited zeal and vigor. They wanted to excel each other in their effort and sacrifice. It was their untiring zeal which brought them to Egypt, Syria, Turkestan, Iran, Iraq, Khorasan, Northern Africa, Spain and India. It appeared that humanity was awakened out of a deep sleep after a lapse of hundreds of years.

The Companions of Prophet Muhammad (saw) had no mission except to please Allah. They traveled from country to country, town to town, village to village and hamlet to hamlet to convey the message of truth. They displayed such humility, piety, purity, love and kindness that even angels envied them. They set new standards of morality, sacrifice and devotion. They embraced those whom society had long forgotten. They taught humanity lessons of equality and justice. They created such an environment that evil and immorality became rare and people developed a deep aversion for wrongdoing. They infused new life into humanity just as rain brings new life to the earth.

Universality and Perfection of Islam

Allah has said in the Holy Quran:

$$\text{ٱلۡيَوۡمَ أَكۡمَلۡتُ لَكُمۡ دِينَكُمۡ وَأَتۡمَمۡتُ عَلَيۡكُمۡ نِعۡمَتِى وَرَضِيتُ لَكُمُ ٱلۡإِسۡلَٰمَ دِينًا}$$

> This day I have perfected for you your religion and completed My favor upon you and have chosen for you Islam as the religion. [Al-Maidah, 5:3]

$$\text{مَّا كَانَ مُحَمَّدٌ أَبَآ أَحَدٍ مِّن رِّجَالِكُمۡ وَلَٰكِن رَّسُولَ ٱللَّهِ وَخَاتَمَ ٱلنَّبِيِّـۧنَ}$$

> Muhammad is not the father of [any] one of your men, but [he is] the Messenger of Allah and last of the prophets. [Al-Ahzab, 33:40]

Very few people ponder over the magnanimity of the great bounty that Allah has bestowed upon the Muslim *ummah* and the entire mankind through these verses. Through these verses, Allah has declared that prophethood has ended with Prophet Muhammad (saw), the divine religion (i.e. Islam) has been perfected, there is no need for any alteration in the divine religion, there is no need for any new prophet to come and there is no room for anyone to claim prophethood.

These declarations contain very profound lessons:

1. The *'aqeedah* and *arkaan*[44] (basic rituals) of Islam will remain unchanged forever.
2. They will remain the same for every part of the world.

Thus the faith as well as the basic rituals of Islam will remain the same across the world until the Last Day. Wherever Muslims will live in whatever period of time, their faith and rituals will remain unaltered.

Universality of *'Aqeedah*

The *'aqeedah* of those who call themselves Muslim, recite Quran and claim Islam to be their religion has remained unchanged since the time of Prophet Muhammad (saw) and will remain so as long as this world remains in existence. *Tawheed*, the coming of all the prophets who were selected and sent by Allah to different regions at different times and the finality of Prophet Muhammad (saw) have always been and will always remain an integral part of the belief system of Muslims. This is what is meant by the universality of *'aqeedah*.

The status of Prophet Muhammad (saw) as the final prophet of Allah is not an ordinary thing; his prophethood is for all times (until the Last Day) and for all regions of the world. Similar is the status of his *ummah*; no previous *ummah* was endowed with the belief system and code of conduct that transcended all time periods and all geographical boundaries.

Universality of *Arkaan*

The *arkaan* of Islam will remain unaltered regardless of time and place. It will never happen that obligatory daily prayers will be reduced from five to three because of some adverse condition, or that the days of obligatory fasting (in the month of *Ramadan*) will be replaced by some other days.

A person once said, "You Muslims fast in such hot days. Why don't you fix *Ramadan* in winter months?" I replied, "*Arkaan* of Islam will never be

---

[44] ارکان - *Salah* (five daily prayers), *saum* (fasting) in the month of Ramadan, *zakah* (obligatory poor-due) and *hajj* (pilgrimage to Makkah)

compromised and they will always be practiced in the same way. Obligatory prayers will always be five. Fasting will always be in the month of *Ramadan* whether it falls in summer or winter. *Zakah* will always be paid as prescribed. All the rituals of *hajj* of *Baitullah* will be performed without any alteration. There will be absolutely no change in these practices." This is what is meant by the universality of *arkaan*.

Finality of Prophethood Guarantees Protection of this *Ummah*

I have thoroughly studied history of religions. I have studied authentic books of Judaism and Christianity. I invite you to do the same. You will find that they are full of contradictions in their belief system and in the practice of their rituals. You will find their historians to be apologetic and remorseful in acknowledging that the followers of those religions could not hold on to the teachings of their prophets for long. You will find that there had never been any religion before Islam whose adherents could preserve the teachings of their prophet for even a few centuries, and in some cases, even for a few decades.

History bears testimony to the fact that none of the religions which came prior to Islam claimed to be the final religion and none of the prophets who came before Prophet Muhammad (saw) claimed to be the final prophet. It was only Islam which declared that it was the final religion and it was only Prophet Muhammad (saw) who declared that he was the final prophet.

In all the religions which preceded Islam, you will clearly find that they are full of ambiguities, inconsistencies and contradictions; what was prohibited in the past became permissible later and vice versa; what was once considered an act of worship became taboo later on. Even the very core beliefs and practices changed over time and varied considerably from region to region. Simply put, those religions experienced instability, vacillations and inconsistencies because they were not destined to be the final message and the final religion.

Since the coming of Prophet Muhammad (saw), many revolutions – political, moral, literary, and scientific – came to the world, but they could not change the core beliefs and principles of Islam. The belief[45] in the

---

[45] Verily, when He intends a thing, His Command is, "be", and it is! [Ya-Sin, 36:82]

Oneness, Might and Power of Allah is still intact. The belief that Allah is the sole Creator, Controller and Sustainer of the universe is still intact. The belief that Allah has no partner is still intact. The belief in all the prophets is still intact.

If anyone ever attempted to introduce an incorrect belief in Islam, he did not succeed. Islam is still pure and fully preserved. *Sunnah* (practices and sayings of Prophet Muhammad) are clearly distinguishable from *bid'ah*[46] (illegitimate innovation) and no one can succeed in legitimizing a *bid'ah* as a *sunnah*. No one can succeed in proving that an act which was a sin before has now become a virtuous deed. No one can adulterate *Tawheed* with *shirk*. The reason Islam has remained unadulterated in its core beliefs and practices is the finality of prophethood.

I have traveled extensively all over the world including Europe, Africa, the Americas and Muslim countries. I visited big cities as well as small villages. I met great scholars as well as ordinary Muslims. I visited mosques and tombs. But I did not find any variation in the basic beliefs and practices of Muslims anywhere in the world.

I prayed in congregation everywhere. I was privileged to lead prayers in some countries as well, but I was never given a guidebook and told that people of that country prayed differently (from how people pray in my home country) and made *wudhu*[47] (washing of hands, face and feet before prayer) differently. I led the prayers in my usual way and the local residents did not feel uneasy about it. I went to visit graves and tombs of pious people, but was never told to bow down or seek their help.

Muslims are living in every part of the world, but they all pray the same way. You can go to Afghanistan, Turkestan, England, Morocco, Egypt, Spain, Russia, China, Japan, Libya, Sudan, Algeria or anywhere else and pray without any confusion and even lead a prayer.

It is All the Blessings of the Finality of Prophethood

It is only the blessing of the finality of prophethood that the core elements of Islamic faith (*Tawheed, salah, saum*[48], *zakah* and *hajj*) have remained

---

[46] بدعة

[47] وضو

[48] صوم (fasting)

fully preserved and unadulterated up to this day. Political turmoil and instability often gripped *Hejaz* (Makkah, Madinah and Jeddah) and made the journey for *hajj* unsafe and risky, but Muslims never stopped going for *hajj*. *Hajj* still enjoys the same status in Islam as before and Muslims are still performing it as before; the number of pilgrims has in fact increased significantly in recent years.

Changes in political climate and regimes did not alter the *arkaan* of Islam. They are still being practiced in the same way as originally instituted. Just a few days ago I returned from *Hejaz* after performing *'umrah*. It is the same *Baitullah*, the same *motaaf* (area surrounding *Baitullah*), the same *Haram Sharif* (Grand Mosque) and the same *tawaaf* (ritual of circling around *Baitullah*) which consists of seven rounds of circumambulation of *Baitullah* in a counterclockwise direction.

The number of times one has to circumambulate *Baitullah* in a *tawaaf* has neither increased nor decreased. Nor has it ever been suggested to modify the order or method of doing it. It is being done in the same way as was shown by the Prophet (saw).

Hypothetically speaking, if Allah wills and a *sahabi*[49], a *taaba'i*[50] (such as Hasan Basri, Imam 'Ali Zainul 'Abedin or Sa'id bin Al Musaib, Owais Qarni) or a famous sage (such as Abdul Qadir Jilani, Junaid Baghdadi, Imam Ghazali, Ibn Taimiya, Khaja Moinuddin Chisti, Fariduddin Ganj Shakar and Mujaddid Alf Thani) came out of his grave, he will not find any alteration in Islam and will find it to be the same as it was in the days of Caliphs Abu Bakr (ra), 'Umar (ra), 'Uthman (ra) and 'Ali (ra). In case he finds something altered or new, that would only be the handiwork of someone's ignorance, negligence and self-service and its legitimacy could not be proven.

Likewise no one can venture to alter the Holy Quran as Allah has Himself promised:

$$إِنَّا نَحْنُ نَزَّلْنَا ٱلذِّكْرَ وَإِنَّا لَهُ لَحَافِظُونَ$$

We have, without doubt, sent down the Message; and We will assuredly guard it (from corruption). [Al-Hijr, 15:9]

---

[49] صحابی – A Companion of the Prophet (saw).
[50] تابعی - Someone who did not see the Prophet (saw), but saw a *sahabi*.

Adulteration in *Shari'ah* is Unforgivable

Allah has perfected Islam. We should be thankful to Him for this great favor. We should value this priceless gift. We should feel proud of being part of this great *ummah*.

We have a complete *Shari'ah* in front of us. It does not need any addition or deletion. If someone dares to make any change to it, he will be deemed disrespectful to Allah and His Prophet (saw). We can proudly say to a follower of any religion that he will find the same *Shari'ah* wherever he goes. He will find the same *arkaan*, rules and regulations in every part of the world. Timings of the obligatory prayers will be the same whether it is London, New York, Moscow or Paris. They will be the same whether one is at home or away from home, whichever season of the year it is, whether the political condition is favorable or not, whether the climate is hot, cold or temperate. There will always be five obligatory prayers in a 24-hour period. In shorter days, it will not be reduced to three. Nor will it be increased to seven in longer days. Nor will the timings of *'Asr*[51] (late afternoon prayer) and *Maghrib*[52] (prayer immediately after sunset) be swapped.

The fact that there has never been any alteration or modification in the basic principles of Islam is nothing but the blessing of the finality of prophethood of Prophet Muhammad (saw).

---

[51] عصر

[52] مغرب

Chapter 3 – The Life Hereafter

Prophets first enlightened mankind with the knowledge of Allah and His attributes. They then brought the knowledge of the Life Hereafter – the life that begins after a person leaves this world. They made mankind aware that the entire universe would be dismantled one day, every soul would be resurrected and every soul would be held accountable for all of its deeds.

The knowledge of the Life Hereafter cannot be acquired through any other source except the prophets. This knowledge is beyond the reach of human faculty - intelligence, experience, power of reasoning and sensory systems. There is no way to get a glimpse of that life from this life. While living in this world, the facts of that life can be neither verified nor disproved.

Humans have only two options with respect to this knowledge. They may rely upon prophets and trust their knowledge. Or, they may reject it because of their insistence on physical evidence. The Holy Quran has mentioned this in the following verse:

قُل لَّا يَعْلَمُ مَن فِى ٱلسَّمَـٰوَٰتِ وَٱلْأَرْضِ ٱلْغَيْبَ إِلَّا ٱللَّهُ وَمَا يَشْعُرُونَ أَيَّانَ يُبْعَثُونَ (65) بَلِ ٱدَّٰرَكَ عِلْمُهُمْ فِى ٱلْآخِرَةِ بَلْ هُمْ فِى شَكٍّ مِّنْهَا بَلْ هُم مِّنْهَا عَمُونَ (66)

Say, "None in the heavens and earth knows the unseen except Allah, and they do not perceive when they will be resurrected." Rather, their knowledge is arrested concerning the Hereafter. Rather, they are in doubt about it. Rather, they are, concerning it, blind. [An-Naml, 27:65-66]

However, there are enough signs and clues for a rational mind to conclude that the Life Hereafter is indeed feasible and there is no logical dilemma in accepting the existence of the life after death.

One of the greatest signs of the existence of the Hereafter is the birth and life of the man himself. He goes through the stages of being a sperm-drop, clot of congealed blood, fetus, bones and flesh[1]. He then comes out of the

---

[1] The Holy Quran vividly describes the phases of human creation in the chapter Al-Muminun (23:13-14)

womb of his mother as a beautiful creation. He remains in the state of childhood before turning into a handsome adult. If he is fortunate enough to survive the spring years of his youth, he enters into the fall season of old age. The clock then starts turning in the reverse direction and his old age starts looking more like the days of his childhood. He becomes fragile and incapacitated. He loses his memory and starts forgetting things and people whom he knew very well. He once again becomes dependent on others for everything like an infant.

When he dies, he finishes just one phase of his long journey which has not yet ended by any means. He has only completed the phase of this world and entered into the next phase that is known as *barzakh*[2] which will last until the Day of Resurrection.

Knowing how he was created out of clay and water and knowing what his beginning was, is it possible to have doubt in how he will be brought back to life again after death? After a person has gone through so many transitions, why does he find it difficult to believe that he will have to go through one more transition?

The other clear sign of the Hereafter is in how the earth gains new life after becoming dead. The earth which carries sustenance for countless humans and animals becomes dead and lifeless during the hot summer[3] (in temperate climate). But the rain that falls from the sky quenches its thirst and the parched land suddenly becomes full of life and vigor. It is as if it has woken up from death and started a new life. Grass turns green. Fruits, flowers, crops and vegetables start sprouting and the whole environment becomes lively and spirited.

Quranic Statements about the Life Hereafter

There is plenty of evidence for the Hereafter which everyone can see, especially those who are knowledgeable in biological and agricultural sciences. That is why the Holy Quran has repeatedly drawn the attention of its readers to two phenomena: 1) How a human body goes through various stages in its formation and 2) How the dead earth becomes fertile after rainfall. Here are some verses of the Holy Quran in this regard:

---

[2] برزخ
[3] Similar phenomenon occurs in winter months in cold regions

يَـٰٓأَيُّهَا ٱلنَّاسُ إِن كُنتُمْ فِى رَيْبٍ مِّنَ ٱلْبَعْثِ فَإِنَّا خَلَقْنَـٰكُم مِّن تُرَابٍ ثُمَّ مِن نُّطْفَةٍ ثُمَّ مِنْ عَلَقَةٍ ثُمَّ مِن مُّضْغَةٍ مُّخَلَّقَةٍ وَغَيْرِ مُخَلَّقَةٍ لِّنُبَيِّنَ لَكُمْ وَنُقِرُّ فِى ٱلْأَرْحَامِ مَا نَشَآءُ إِلَىٰٓ أَجَلٍ مُّسَمًّى ثُمَّ نُخْرِجُكُمْ طِفْلًا ثُمَّ لِتَبْلُغُوٓا۟ أَشُدَّكُمْ وَمِنكُم مَّن يُتَوَفَّىٰ وَمِنكُم مَّن يُرَدُّ إِلَىٰٓ أَرْذَلِ ٱلْعُمُرِ لِكَيْلَا يَعْلَمَ مِنۢ بَعْدِ عِلْمٍ شَيْئًا وَتَرَى ٱلْأَرْضَ هَامِدَةً فَإِذَآ أَنزَلْنَا عَلَيْهَا ٱلْمَآءَ ٱهْتَزَّتْ وَرَبَتْ وَأَنۢبَتَتْ مِن كُلِّ زَوْجٍ بَهِيجٍ (5) ذَٰلِكَ بِأَنَّ ٱللَّهَ هُوَ ٱلْحَقُّ وَأَنَّهُۥ يُحْىِ ٱلْمَوْتَىٰ وَأَنَّهُۥ عَلَىٰ كُلِّ شَىْءٍ قَدِيرٌ (6) وَأَنَّ ٱلسَّاعَةَ ءَاتِيَةٌ لَّا رَيْبَ فِيهَا وَأَنَّ ٱللَّهَ يَبْعَثُ مَن فِى ٱلْقُبُورِ (7)

O mankind! If you have a doubt about the Resurrection, (consider) that We created you out of dust, then out of sperm, then out of a leech-like clot, then out of a morsel of flesh, partly formed and partly unformed, in order that We may manifest (our power) to you; and We cause whom We will to rest in the wombs for an appointed term, then do We bring you out as babes, then (foster you) that you may reach your age of full strength; and some of you are called to die, and some are sent back to the feeblest old age, so that they know nothing after having known (much), and (further), you see the earth barren and lifeless, but when We pour down rain on it, it is stirred (to life), it swells, and it puts forth every kind of beautiful growth (in pairs). This is so, because Allah is the Reality. It is He Who gives life to the dead, and it is He Who has power over all things. And verily the Hour will come. There can be no doubt about it or about (the fact) that Allah will bring up all who are in the graves. [Al-Hajj, 22:5-7]

وَلَقَدْ خَلَقْنَا ٱلْإِنسَـٰنَ مِن سُلَـٰلَةٍ مِّن طِينٍ (12) ثُمَّ جَعَلْنَـٰهُ نُطْفَةً فِى قَرَارٍ مَّكِينٍ (13) ثُمَّ خَلَقْنَا ٱلنُّطْفَةَ عَلَقَةً فَخَلَقْنَا ٱلْعَلَقَةَ مُضْغَةً فَخَلَقْنَا ٱلْمُضْغَةَ عِظَـٰمًا فَكَسَوْنَا ٱلْعِظَـٰمَ لَحْمًا ثُمَّ أَنشَأْنَـٰهُ خَلْقًا ءَاخَرَ فَتَبَارَكَ ٱللَّهُ أَحْسَنُ ٱلْخَـٰلِقِينَ (14) ثُمَّ إِنَّكُم بَعْدَ ذَٰلِكَ لَمَيِّتُونَ (15) ثُمَّ إِنَّكُمْ يَوْمَ ٱلْقِيَـٰمَةِ تُبْعَثُونَ (16)

We did create man from a quintessence (of clay). Then We placed him as (a drop of) sperm in a place of rest, firmly fixed. Then We made the sperm into a clot of congealed blood; then of that clot We made a (fetus) lump; then we made out of that lump bones and clothed the bones with flesh; then we developed out of it another creature. So blessed be Allah, the best to create! After that, you will certainly die. Again, on the Day of Judgment, you will be raised up. [Al-Muminun, 23:12-16]

اللَّهُ ٱلَّذِى يُرْسِلُ ٱلرِّيَـٰحَ فَتُثِيرُ سَحَابًا فَيَبْسُطُهُ فِى ٱلسَّمَآءِ كَيْفَ يَشَآءُ وَيَجْعَلُهُ كِسَفًا فَتَرَى ٱلْوَدْقَ يَخْرُجُ مِنْ خِلَـٰلِهِۦ فَإِذَآ أَصَابَ بِهِۦ مَن يَشَآءُ مِنْ عِبَادِهِۦٓ إِذَا هُمْ يَسْتَبْشِرُونَ (48) وَإِن كَانُوا۟ مِن قَبْلِ أَن يُنَزَّلَ عَلَيْهِم مِّن قَبْلِهِۦ لَمُبْلِسِينَ (49) فَٱنظُرْ إِلَىٰٓ ءَاثَـٰرِ رَحْمَتِ ٱللَّهِ كَيْفَ يُحْىِ ٱلْأَرْضَ بَعْدَ مَوْتِهَآ إِنَّ ذَٰلِكَ لَمُحْىِ ٱلْمَوْتَىٰ وَهُوَ عَلَىٰ كُلِّ شَىْءٍ قَدِيرٌ (50)

Allah is the One who sends the winds, so they stir up a cloud. He then spreads it in the sky however He wills, and makes it (split) into pieces. Then you see the rain coming out from its midst. So, once He makes it reach those whom He wills from His slaves, they start rejoicing, even though they were absolutely hopeless before it was sent down to them. So, look to the effects of Allah's mercy, how He gives life to the earth after its death. Surely, Allah is the One who will give life to the dead; and He has the power to do everything. [Ar-Rum, 30:48-50]

وَٱللَّهُ ٱلَّذِىٓ أَرْسَلَ ٱلرِّيَـٰحَ فَتُثِيرُ سَحَابًا فَسُقْنَـٰهُ إِلَىٰ بَلَدٍ مَّيِّتٍ فَأَحْيَيْنَا بِهِ ٱلْأَرْضَ بَعْدَ مَوْتِهَا كَذَٰلِكَ ٱلنُّشُورُ

It is Allah Who sends forth the winds, so that they raise up the clouds, and drive them to a land that is dead, and revive the earth therewith after its death: even so (will be) the Resurrection! [Fatir, 35:9]

وَمِنْ ءَايَـٰتِهِۦٓ أَنَّكَ تَرَى ٱلْأَرْضَ خَـٰشِعَةً فَإِذَآ أَنزَلْنَا عَلَيْهَا ٱلْمَآءَ ٱهْتَزَّتْ وَرَبَتْ إِنَّ ٱلَّذِىٓ أَحْيَاهَا لَمُحْىِ ٱلْمَوْتَىٰٓ إِنَّهُۥ عَلَىٰ كُلِّ شَىْءٍ قَدِيرٌ

And among His Signs is this; you see the earth barren and desolate, but when We send down rain to it, it is stirred to life and yields increase. Truly, He Who gives life to the (dead) earth can surely give life to (men) who are dead. He has power over all things. [Fussilat, 41:39]

وَٱلَّذِى نَزَّلَ مِنَ ٱلسَّمَآءِ مَآءً بِقَدَرٍ فَأَنشَرْنَا بِهِ بَلْدَةً مَّيْتًا كَذَٰلِكَ تُخْرَجُونَ

We send down (from time to time) rain from the sky in due measure and We raise to life therewith a land that is dead; in the same way, you will be brought forth (alive from the graves). [Az-Zukhraf, 43:11]

Other Signs of the Life Hereafter

Besides these two signs (formation of the human body in a womb and reinvigoration of the earth by rainfall), there are many other signs which point to the Life Hereafter and are in display day and night in front of our eyes.

Anyone who ponders over how things were created initially from nothing and studies how precisely and meticulously the reproductive system works cannot doubt the life after death, even for a moment. The Holy Quran alludes to this fact in the following verses:

أَوَلَمْ يَرَوْاْ كَيْفَ يُبْدِئُ ٱللَّهُ ٱلْخَلْقَ ثُمَّ يُعِيدُهُ إِنَّ ذَٰلِكَ عَلَى ٱللَّهِ يَسِيرٌ (19) قُلْ سِيرُواْ فِى ٱلْأَرْضِ فَٱنظُرُواْ كَيْفَ بَدَأَ ٱلْخَلْقَ ثُمَّ ٱللَّهُ يُنشِئُ ٱلنَّشْأَةَ ٱلْآخِرَةَ إِنَّ ٱللَّهَ عَلَىٰ كُلِّ شَىْءٍ قَدِيرٌ (20)

Have they not considered how Allah begins creation and then repeats it? Indeed that, for Allah, is easy. Say, [O Muhammad], "Travel through the land and observe how He began creation. Then Allah will produce the final creation. Indeed, Allah has the power to do everything." [Al-Ankabut, 29:19-20]

يُخْرِجُ ٱلْحَىَّ مِنَ ٱلْمَيِّتِ وَيُخْرِجُ ٱلْمَيِّتَ مِنَ ٱلْحَىِّ وَيُحْىِ ٱلْأَرْضَ بَعْدَ مَوْتِهَا وَكَذَٰلِكَ تُخْرَجُونَ

He brings the living out of the dead and brings the dead out of the living and brings to life the earth after its lifelessness. And thus will you be brought out. [Ar-Rum, 30:19]

Even for humans, reproducing an object is usually easier than creating it for the first instance. Then why should it be difficult for Allah to resurrect humans after their death? For Allah, recreating things is as easy as creating them for the first time from nothing, as He has mentioned in the Holy Quran:

وَهُوَ ٱلَّذِى يَبْدَؤُاْ ٱلْخَلْقَ ثُمَّ يُعِيدُهُ وَهُوَ أَهْوَنُ عَلَيْهِ وَلَهُ ٱلْمَثَلُ ٱلْأَعْلَىٰ فِى ٱلسَّمَٰوَٰتِ وَٱلْأَرْضِ وَهُوَ ٱلْعَزِيزُ ٱلْحَكِيمُ

It is He Who begins (the process of) creation; then repeats it; and for Him it is most easy. To Him belongs the loftiest similitude (we can think of) in the heavens and the earth; He is the Exalted in might, full of wisdom. [Ar-Rum, 30:27]

أَوَلَمْ يَرَ ٱلْإِنسَٰنُ أَنَّا خَلَقْنَٰهُ مِن نُّطْفَةٍ فَإِذَا هُوَ خَصِيمٌ مُّبِينٌ (77) وَضَرَبَ لَنَا مَثَلاً وَنَسِيَ خَلْقَهُ قَالَ مَن يُحْيِ ٱلْعِظَٰمَ وَهِىَ رَمِيمٌ (78) قُلْ يُحْيِيهَا ٱلَّذِى أَنشَأَهَا أَوَّلَ مَرَّةٍ وَهُوَ بِكُلِّ خَلْقٍ عَلِيمٌ (79) ٱلَّذِى جَعَلَ لَكُم مِّنَ ٱلشَّجَرِ ٱلْأَخْضَرِ نَارًا فَإِذَا أَنتُم مِّنْهُ تُوقِدُونَ (80) أَوَلَيْسَ ٱلَّذِى خَلَقَ ٱلسَّمَٰوَٰتِ وَٱلْأَرْضَ بِقَٰدِرٍ عَلَىٰ أَن يَخْلُقَ مِثْلَهُم بَلَىٰ وَهُوَ ٱلْخَلَّٰقُ ٱلْعَلِيمُ (81) إِنَّمَآ أَمْرُهُ إِذَآ أَرَادَ شَيْئًا أَن يَقُولَ لَهُ كُن فَيَكُونُ (82) فَسُبْحَٰنَ ٱلَّذِى بِيَدِهِ مَلَكُوتُ كُلِّ شَىْءٍ وَإِلَيْهِ تُرْجَعُونَ (83)

Did man not see that We have created him from a drop of sperm? Then suddenly he stood up as an open adversary (to Us). He has set up an argument about Us and forgot his own creation. He said, "Who will give life to the bones when they are decayed?" Say, these will be revived by the same One who had created them for the first time and who is fully aware of every creation, the One who created for you fire from the green tree, and in no time you kindle from it. Is it that the One who has created the heavens and the earth has no power to create ones like them? Why not?

He is the Supreme Creator, the All-Knowing. Verily, when He intends a thing, His Command is, "be", and it is! So glory to Him in whose hands is the dominion of all things; and to Him will you be all brought back. [Ya-Sin, 36:77-83]

وَٱللَّهُ أَنْبَتَكُم مِّنَ ٱلْأَرْضِ نَبَاتًا (17) ثُمَّ يُعِيدُكُمْ فِيهَا وَيُخْرِجُكُمْ إِخْرَاجًا (18)

And Allah has created you from the earth growing (gradually). And in the end He will return you into the (earth), and raise you forth (again at the Resurrection). [Nuh, 71:17-18]

أَوَلَمْ يَرَوْاْ أَنَّ ٱللَّهَ ٱلَّذِى خَلَقَ ٱلسَّمَٰوَٰتِ وَٱلْأَرْضَ وَلَمْ يَعْىَ بِخَلْقِهِنَّ بِقَٰدِرٍ عَلَىٰٓ أَن يُحْىِىَ ٱلْمَوْتَىٰ بَلَىٰٓ إِنَّهُ عَلَىٰ كُلِّ شَىْءٍ قَدِيرٌ

Have they not seen that Allah who has created the heavens and the earth, and was not wearied by their creation, does have power to give life to the dead? Yes of course, He is able to do everything. [Al-Ahqaf, 46:33]

أَفَلَمْ يَنظُرُوٓاْ إِلَى ٱلسَّمَآءِ فَوْقَهُمْ كَيْفَ بَنَيْنَٰهَا وَزَيَّنَّٰهَا وَمَا لَهَا مِن فُرُوجٍ (6) وَٱلْأَرْضَ مَدَدْنَٰهَا وَأَلْقَيْنَا فِيهَا رَوَٰسِىَ وَأَنۢبَتْنَا فِيهَا مِن كُلِّ زَوْجٍ بَهِيجٍ (7) تَبْصِرَةً وَذِكْرَىٰ لِكُلِّ عَبْدٍ مُّنِيبٍ (8) وَنَزَّلْنَا مِنَ ٱلسَّمَآءِ مَآءً مُّبَٰرَكًا فَأَنۢبَتْنَا بِهِۦ جَنَّٰتٍ وَحَبَّ ٱلْحَصِيدِ (9) وَٱلنَّخْلَ بَاسِقَٰتٍ لَّهَا طَلْعٌ نَّضِيدٌ (10) رِّزْقًا لِّلْعِبَادِ وَأَحْيَيْنَا بِهِۦ بَلْدَةً مَّيْتًا كَذَٰلِكَ ٱلْخُرُوجُ (11)

Did they not look at the sky above them, how We have built and beautified it, and it has no cracks? As for the earth, We have spread it out and set thereon mountains standing firm and produced therein every kind of beautiful growth; to be observed and commemorated by every devotee turning (to Allah). And We sent down blessed water from the sky and caused to grow therewith gardens and grain of harvest and towering date palms with shoots of fruit-stalks piled one over another as sustenance for

(Allah's) servants. And We give (new) life therewith to the land that is dead. Thus will be the Resurrection. [Qaf, 50:6-11]

نَحْنُ خَلَقْنَـٰكُمْ فَلَوْلَا تُصَدِّقُونَ (57) أَفَرَءَيْتُم مَّا تُمْنُونَ (58) ءَأَنتُمْ تَخْلُقُونَهُ أَمْ نَحْنُ ٱلْخَـٰلِقُونَ (59) نَحْنُ قَدَّرْنَا بَيْنَكُمُ ٱلْمَوْتَ وَمَا نَحْنُ بِمَسْبُوقِينَ (60) عَلَىٰٓ أَن نُّبَدِّلَ أَمْثَـٰلَكُمْ وَنُنشِئَكُمْ فِى مَا لَا تَعْلَمُونَ (61) وَلَقَدْ عَلِمْتُمُ ٱلنَّشْأَةَ ٱلْأُولَىٰ فَلَوْلَا تَذَكَّرُونَ (62) أَفَرَءَيْتُم مَّا تَحْرُثُونَ (63) ءَأَنتُمْ تَزْرَعُونَهُ أَمْ نَحْنُ ٱلزَّٰرِعُونَ (64) لَوْ نَشَآءُ لَجَعَلْنَـٰهُ حُطَـٰمًا فَظَلْتُمْ تَفَكَّهُونَ (65) إِنَّا لَمُغْرَمُونَ (66) بَلْ نَحْنُ مَحْرُومُونَ (67) أَفَرَءَيْتُمُ ٱلْمَآءَ ٱلَّذِى تَشْرَبُونَ (68) ءَأَنتُمْ أَنزَلْتُمُوهُ مِنَ ٱلْمُزْنِ أَمْ نَحْنُ ٱلْمُنزِلُونَ (69) لَوْ نَشَآءُ جَعَلْنَـٰهُ أُجَاجًا فَلَوْلَا تَشْكُرُونَ (70) أَفَرَءَيْتُمُ ٱلنَّارَ ٱلَّتِى تُورُونَ (71) ءَأَنتُمْ أَنشَأْتُمْ شَجَرَتَهَآ أَمْ نَحْنُ ٱلْمُنشِـُٔونَ (72)

We have created you, so why do you not believe? Have you seen that which you emit? Is it you who creates it, or are We the Creator? We have decreed death among you, and We are not to be outdone. In that We will change your likenesses and produce you in that [form] which you do not know. And you have already known the first creation, so will you not remember? And have you seen that [seed] which you sow? Is it you who makes it grow, or are We the grower? If We willed, We could make it [dry] debris, and you would remain in wonder, [Saying], "Indeed, we are [now] in debt; Rather, we have been deprived." And have you seen the water that you drink? Is it you who brought it down from the clouds, or is it We who bring it down? If We willed, We could make it bitter, so why are you not grateful? And have you seen the fire that you ignite? Is it you who produced its tree, or are We the producer? [Al-Waqi'ah, 56:57-72]

أَيَحْسَبُ ٱلْإِنسَـٰنُ أَن يُتْرَكَ سُدًى (36) أَلَمْ يَكُ نُطْفَةً مِّن مَّنِىٍّ يُمْنَىٰ (37) ثُمَّ كَانَ عَلَقَةً فَخَلَقَ فَسَوَّىٰ (38) فَجَعَلَ مِنْهُ ٱلزَّوْجَيْنِ ٱلذَّكَرَ وَٱلْأُنثَىٰٓ (39) أَلَيْسَ ذَٰلِكَ بِقَـٰدِرٍ عَلَىٰٓ أَن يُحْـِۧىَ ٱلْمَوْتَىٰ (40)

Does man think that he will be left uncontrolled, (without purpose)? Was he not a drop of sperm emitted (in lowly form)? Then did he become a leech-like clot; then did (Allah) make and fashion (him) in due proportion. And of him He made two sexes, male and female. Has not He the power to give life to the dead? [Al-Qiyamah, 75:36-40]

A thoughtful look at the universe and its components is sure to stir a feeling that the current life must have a sequel in which the outcome of this life will come to fruition; otherwise, this life and all of its makings are meaningless and without any purpose. This is what the Holy Quran has alluded to in the following verses:

أَيَحْسَبُ ٱلْإِنسَـٰنُ أَن يُتْرَكَ سُدًى

Does man think that he will be left uncontrolled, (without purpose)? [Al-Qiyamah, 75:36]

أَفَحَسِبْتُمْ أَنَّمَا خَلَقْنَـٰكُمْ عَبَثًا وَأَنَّكُمْ إِلَيْنَا لَا تُرْجَعُونَ

Did you then think that We had created you in jest, and that you would not be brought back to Us (for account)? [Al-Muminun, 23:115]

About the earth and sky, Allah says:

وَمَا خَلَقْنَا ٱلسَّمَآءَ وَٱلْأَرْضَ وَمَا بَيْنَهُمَا بَـٰطِلاً

Not without purpose did We create the sky and earth and all between. [Sad, 38:27]

وَمَا خَلَقْنَا ٱلسَّمَـٰوَٰتِ وَٱلْأَرْضَ وَمَا بَيْنَهُمَا لَـٰعِبِينَ

We created not the skies, the earth, and all between them, merely in (idle) sport. [Ad-Dukhan, 44:38]

If a person ponders over the earth, the sky and their wonders, he precipitously utters the words of astonishment, as the Holy Quran has mentioned:

إِنَّ فِى خَلْقِ ٱلسَّمَٰوَٰتِ وَٱلْأَرْضِ وَٱخْتِلَٰفِ ٱلَّيْلِ وَٱلنَّهَارِ لَأَيَٰتٍ لِّأُوْلِى ٱلْأَلْبَٰبِ (190) ٱلَّذِينَ يَذْكُرُونَ ٱللَّهَ قِيَٰمًا وَقُعُودًا وَعَلَىٰ جُنُوبِهِمْ وَيَتَفَكَّرُونَ فِى خَلْقِ ٱلسَّمَٰوَٰتِ وَٱلْأَرْضِ رَبَّنَا مَا خَلَقْتَ هَٰذَا بَٰطِلاً سُبْحَٰنَكَ فَقِنَا عَذَابَ ٱلنَّارِ (191) رَبَّنَا إِنَّكَ مَن تُدْخِلِ ٱلنَّارَ فَقَدْ أَخْزَيْتَهُ وَمَا لِلظَّٰلِمِينَ مِنْ أَنصَارٍ (192)

Indeed, in the creation of the heavens and the earth and the alternation of the night and the day are signs for those who understand and remember Allah while standing or sitting or [lying] on their sides and give thought to the creation of the heavens and the earth, [saying], "Our Lord, You did not create this aimlessly; exalted are You [above such a thing]; then protect us from the punishment of the Fire. Our Lord, indeed whoever You admit to the Fire - You have disgraced him, and for the wrongdoers there are no helpers." [Al-Imran, 3:190-192]

Difference between those who Believe in the Life Hereafter and those who don't

A firm *'aqeedah* is like a healthy and robust seed. When such a belief is planted in a receptive heart and is properly nourished, it gives birth to a plant which grows into a huge tree that encompasses the entire life of a person.

The belief in the Life Hereafter is a seed which has its own characteristics. When it is nurtured properly, it breeds good character and affects every aspect of human life. The difference between those who believe in the Hereafter and those who do not is the same as the difference between the trees which are born out of healthy seeds and those which are the product of unhealthy seeds. Their attitude, thinking, behavior and lifestyle are quite different. It appears that they have been cast out of different molds.

The fundamental difference between the one who believes in the Hereafter and the one who does not is that the former chooses to wait for the benefit to come to him later whereas the latter wants to have it right away; the former opts for eternal reward whereas the latter settles only for the temporary and immediate return. The Holy Quran repeatedly draws attention to this difference; it terms the pleasure of this life as transitory and that of the Hereafter as permanent and prods a person to make his selection out of the two:

مَّن كَانَ يُرِيدُ ٱلْعَاجِلَةَ عَجَّلْنَا لَهُ فِيهَا مَا نَشَآءُ لِمَن نُّرِيدُ ثُمَّ جَعَلْنَا لَهُ جَهَنَّمَ يَصْلَلَهَا مَذْمُومًا مَّدْحُورًا (18) وَمَنْ أَرَادَ ٱلْآخِرَةَ وَسَعَىٰ لَهَا سَعْيَهَا وَهُوَ مُؤْمِنٌ فَأُوْلَٰٓئِكَ كَانَ سَعْيُهُم مَّشْكُورًا (19)

To anyone who desires the harvest of the Hereafter, We give increase in his harvest, and to anyone who desires the harvest of this world, We grant somewhat thereof, but he has no share in the Hereafter. [Ash-Shura, 42:20]

Those who do not believe in the Hereafter are hasty in nature, as the Holy Quran mentions:

كَلَّا بَلْ تُحِبُّونَ ٱلْعَاجِلَةَ (20) وَتَذَرُونَ ٱلْآخِرَةَ (21)

بركة ⁴

No! But you love the immediate. And leave the Hereafter.
[Al-Qiyamah, 75:20-21]

إِنَّ هَـٰٓؤُلَآءِ يُحِبُّونَ ٱلۡعَاجِلَةَ وَيَذَرُونَ وَرَآءَهُمۡ يَوۡمًا ثَقِيلًا

In fact these people love that which is immediate, and
neglect a Heavy Day ahead of them. [Al-Insan, 76:27]

فَخَلَفَ مِنۢ بَعۡدِهِمۡ خَلۡفٌ وَرِثُواْ ٱلۡكِتَـٰبَ يَأۡخُذُونَ عَرَضَ هَـٰذَا
ٱلۡأَدۡنَىٰ وَيَقُولُونَ سَيُغۡفَرُ لَنَا وَإِن يَأۡتِهِمۡ عَرَضٌ مِّثۡلُهُۥ يَأۡخُذُوهُ أَلَمۡ
يُؤۡخَذۡ عَلَيۡهِم مِّيثَـٰقُ ٱلۡكِتَـٰبِ أَن لَّا يَقُولُواْ عَلَى ٱللَّهِ إِلَّا ٱلۡحَقَّ
وَدَرَسُواْ مَا فِيهِۗ وَٱلدَّارُ ٱلۡأَخِرَةُ خَيۡرٌ لِّلَّذِينَ يَتَّقُونَۚ أَفَلَا تَعۡقِلُونَ

Then, after them, came a generation which inherited the
Book, opting for the vanities of this world and saying we
shall be forgiven. If there comes to them similar stuff, they
would opt for it (again). Was not the covenant of the Book
taken from them that they should not say anything but the
truth about Allah? They learnt what it contained.
Certainly, the last abode is better for those who fear Allah.
Have you then, no sense? [Al-A'raf, 7:169]

There is a huge difference between the thinking and mindset of these two
kinds of people, as the Holy Quran mentions:

فَإِذَا قَضَيۡتُم مَّنَـٰسِكَكُمۡ فَٱذۡكُرُواْ ٱللَّهَ كَذِكۡرِكُمۡ ءَابَآءَكُمۡ أَوۡ أَشَدَّ
ذِكۡرًاۗ فَمِنَ ٱلنَّاسِ مَن يَقُولُ رَبَّنَآ ءَاتِنَا فِى ٱلدُّنۡيَا وَمَا لَهُۥ فِى
ٱلۡأَخِرَةِ مِنۡ خَلَـٰقٍ (200) وَمِنۡهُم مَّن يَقُولُ رَبَّنَآ ءَاتِنَا فِى ٱلدُّنۡيَا
حَسَنَةً وَفِى ٱلۡأَخِرَةِ حَسَنَةً وَقِنَا عَذَابَ ٱلنَّارِ (201)

And among the people is he who says, "Our Lord, give us
in this world," and he will have in the Hereafter no share.
But among them is he who says, "Our Lord, give us in this
world [that which is] good and in the Hereafter [that
which is] good and protect us from the punishment of the
Fire." [Al-Baqarah, 2:200-201]

They have very different views of this life. One says:

يَٰقَوْمِ إِنَّمَا هَٰذِهِ ٱلْحَيَوٰةُ ٱلدُّنْيَا مَتَٰعٌ وَإِنَّ ٱلْآخِرَةَ هِىَ دَارُ ٱلْقَرَارِ

O my people! This life of the present is nothing but (temporary) convenience. It is the Hereafter that is the Home that will last. [Ghafir, 40:39]

Whereas the other says:

إِنْ هِىَ إِلَّا حَيَاتُنَا ٱلدُّنْيَا نَمُوتُ وَنَحْيَا وَمَا نَحْنُ بِمَبْعُوثِينَ

There is nothing but the life in this world! We shall die and we shall live! But we shall never be raised up again! [Al-Muminun, 23:37]

Belief in the Life Hereafter inhibits arrogance, lust of personal glory, and wishing evil, mischief and unrest in the world, as the Holy Quran mentions:

تِلْكَ ٱلدَّارُ ٱلْآخِرَةُ نَجْعَلُهَا لِلَّذِينَ لَا يُرِيدُونَ عُلُوًّا فِى ٱلْأَرْضِ وَلَا فَسَادًا ۚ وَٱلْعَٰقِبَةُ لِلْمُتَّقِينَ

That Home of the Hereafter We shall give to those who intend not high-handedness or mischief on earth and the end is (best) for the righteous. [Al-Qasas, 28:83]

That is why a person who believes in the Hereafter does not aspire for personal glory and remains humble even in a position of authority and power. The more he rises in worldly stature, the more humble he becomes. Abundance of power and wealth does not entice him to declare as Qarun[5] proclaimed, "I have got it due to my knowledge and skill" [Al-Qasas, 28:78]. Rather, he says what Prophet Sulaiman[6] (*alaihis salaam*) said, "This is by the Grace of my Lord to test me whether I am grateful or not" [An-Naml, 27:40].

When a person who believes in the Hereafter is blessed with a vast kingdom, he does not boast like Pharaoh who said, "O my people! Does not the dominion of Egypt belong to me and are these streams not flowing

---

[5] Qarun possessed a huge amount of wealth at the time of Prophet Musa.
[6] Known as Solomon in Western literature

underneath my (palace)?" [Az-Zukhraf, 43:51]; and he does not proclaim, "Who is superior to us in strength? [Fussilat, 41:15]

Instead, he finds his heart filled with the praise of Almighty Allah and says as Prophet Sulaiman (*alaihis salaam*) said:

فَتَبَسَّمَ ضَاحِكًا مِّن قَوْلِهَا وَقَالَ رَبِّ أَوْزِعْنِىٓ أَنْ أَشْكُرَ نِعْمَتَكَ ٱلَّتِىٓ أَنْعَمْتَ عَلَىَّ وَعَلَىٰ وَٰلِدَىَّ وَأَنْ أَعْمَلَ صَٰلِحًا تَرْضَىٰهُ وَأَدْخِلْنِى بِرَحْمَتِكَ فِى عِبَادِكَ ٱلصَّٰلِحِينَ

> O my Lord! Enable me so that I may be grateful for Your favors, which You have bestowed on me and on my parents, and that I may work the righteousness that will please You. And admit me, by Your Grace, to the ranks of Your righteous servants. [An-Naml, 27:19]

He does not feel content with the luxuries and kingdom of this world. He knows that the real honor lies in the Hereafter and true wealth is the obedience of Allah. That is why he shows gratitude to Allah for all of His favors and his ultimate wish is to depart from this world as one of His truly obedient slaves, as Prophet Yusuf (*alaihis salaam*) had wished:

رَبِّ قَدْ ءَاتَيْتَنِى مِنَ ٱلْمُلْكِ وَعَلَّمْتَنِى مِن تَأْوِيلِ ٱلْأَحَادِيثِ فَاطِرَ ٱلسَّمَٰوَٰتِ وَٱلْأَرْضِ أَنتَ وَلِىِّ فِى ٱلدُّنْيَا وَٱلْأَخِرَةِ تَوَفَّنِى مُسْلِمًا وَأَلْحِقْنِى بِٱلصَّٰلِحِينَ

> O my Lord! You have indeed bestowed on me some power and taught me something of the interpretation of dreams and events. O You the Creator of the heavens and the earth! You are my Protector in this world and in the Hereafter. Take my soul (at death) as the one submitting to Your will (as a Muslim), and unite me with the righteous ones. [Yusuf, 12:101]

He is more worried about being disgraced in the Hereafter than in this world. He shivers with the fear of being condemned in the Hereafter, as Prophet Ibrahim (*alaihis salaam*) expressed in his supplication:

وَلَا تُخْزِنِى يَوْمَ يُبْعَثُونَ (87) يَوْمَ لَا يَنفَعُ مَالٌ وَلَا بَنُونَ (88) إِلَّا مَنْ أَتَى ٱللَّهَ بِقَلْبٍ سَلِيمٍ (89)

And let me not be in disgrace on the Day when (men) will be raised up on the Day wherein neither wealth nor children will be of any avail. But only he (will prosper) who brings to Allah a sound heart. [Ash-Sh'uara, 26:87-89]

D'ua of a Momin

The following verse of the Holy Quran exemplifies *d'ua* (supplication) of a *momin* (believer):

رَبَّنَآ إِنَّكَ مَن تُدْخِلِ ٱلنَّارَ فَقَدْ أَخْزَيْتَهُ ۖ وَمَا لِلظَّٰلِمِينَ مِنْ أَنصَارٍ (192) رَبَّنَآ إِنَّنَا سَمِعْنَا مُنَادِيًا يُنَادِى لِلْإِيمَٰنِ أَنْ ءَامِنُواْ بِرَبِّكُمْ فَـَٔامَنَّا ۚ رَبَّنَا فَٱغْفِرْ لَنَا ذُنُوبَنَا وَكَفِّرْ عَنَّا سَيِّـَٔاتِنَا وَتَوَفَّنَا مَعَ ٱلْأَبْرَارِ (193) رَبَّنَا وَءَاتِنَا مَا وَعَدتَّنَا عَلَىٰ رُسُلِكَ وَلَا تُخْزِنَا يَوْمَ ٱلْقِيَٰمَةِ ۗ إِنَّكَ لَا تُخْلِفُ ٱلْمِيعَادَ (194)

Our Lord! Indeed whoever You admit to the Fire, You have disgraced him, and for the wrongdoers there are no helpers. Our Lord! Indeed we have heard a caller calling to faith, [saying], "Believe in your Lord," and we have believed. Our Lord! Forgive our sins and remove from us our misdeeds and cause us to die with the righteous ones. Our Lord! Grant us what You promised us through Your messengers and do not disgrace us on the Day of Resurrection. Indeed, You do not fail in [Your] promise. [Al-Imran, 3:192-194]

That is why a believer is willing to endure all kinds of hardship, punishment and disgrace in this life to save himself from the torments of the Hereafter. This is the fear that exhorts him to voluntarily present himself for punishment in this life for his wrongdoings to avoid punishment in the Hereafter for the same.

In the days of Prophet Muhammad (saw), a Muslim man (Ma'iz b. Malik al-Aslami) and a Muslim woman (from the Ghamid tribe) repeatedly confessed of having committed adultery and desired that they be punished in this life so that they were saved from the disgrace and punishment of the Hereafter. This incident is reported in *Sahih Muslim* (*Kitabul Hudud*) as follows:

'Abdullah b. Buraida reported on the authority of his father that Ma'iz b. Malik al-Aslami came to Allah's Messenger and said, "Allah's Messenger, I have wronged myself. I have committed adultery and I earnestly desire that you should purify me." The Messenger of Allah turned him away. On the following day, he (Ma'iz) again came to the Messenger and said, "I have committed adultery." Allah's Messenger turned him away for the second time, called people of his tribe and asked, "Do you know if there is anything wrong with his mind?" They denied any such thing in him and said, "We do not know him but as a wise good man among us, so far as we can judge." He (Ma'iz) came for the third time. Allah's Messenger sent him back as he had done before and inquired of the people of his tribe if there was anything wrong with him. They informed Allah's Messenger that there was nothing wrong with him or with his mind. When he came for the fourth time, a ditch was dug for him and he (Allah's Messenger) pronounced judgment about him and he was stoned.

The narrator further said, "There came to Allah's Messenger a woman from the tribe of Ghamid and said, "Allah's Messenger, I have committed adultery, so purify me." The Prophet turned her away. On the following day she came again and said, "O Allah's Messenger! Why do you turn me away? Perhaps, you turn me away as you turned away Ma'iz. By Allah, I have become pregnant." The Prophet said, "Well, if you insist upon it, then go away until you give birth to (the child)." After she delivered the child, she came to the Prophet with the child (wrapped) in a rag and said, "Here is the child whom I have given birth to." The Prophet said, "Go away and suckle him until he starts eating." After the child started eating, she came back to the Prophet with the child holding a piece of bread in his hand and said, "I have stopped him nursing and he now eats food." The Prophet entrusted the child to one of the Muslims and then pronounced punishment for her. She was put in a ditch up to her chest and the Prophet commanded people to stone her. Khalid bin Walid came forward with a stone and flung it at her head. The blood that spurted out of her head fell on the face of Khalid upon which he uttered some harsh words. Upon hearing what Khalid had said, the Prophet said to Khalid, "Do not utter bad words about her. By Him in Whose Hand is my life, she has made such a repentance that even if a wrongful tax-collector were to repent, he would have been forgiven." Thereafter, her funeral prayer was performed and she was buried.

The person who does not believe in the Hereafter and whose sole objective is this life will deem the above conduct as purely irrational and extremely fanatical. But for a person who believes in the Hereafter, nothing could be wiser than this because the punishment of the Hereafter is much more severe, painful and disgraceful than the punishment of this world, as the Holy Quran mentions:

$$\text{وَلَعَذَابُ ٱلْأَخِرَةِ أَشَدُّ وَأَبْقَىٰ}$$

And the punishment of the Hereafter is more severe and more lasting. [Ta-Ha, 20:127]

$$\text{وَلَعَذَابُ ٱلْأَخِرَةِ أَخْزَىٰ}$$

The punishment of the Hereafter is more disgraceful. [Fussilat, 41:16]

$$\text{وَلَعَذَابُ ٱلْأَخِرَةِ أَشَقُّ وَمَا لَهُم مِّنَ ٱللَّهِ مِن وَاقٍ}$$

The punishment of the Hereafter is more severe and there will be no one to protect them from the wrath of Allah. [Ar-R'ad, 13:34]

Effects of Belief in the Hereafter

The effect of belief in the Hereafter is that a person remains equally vigilant both in public and private and refrains from committing any wrong even if no one is watching him.

In the Battle of Qadisiyah (15 AH, 636 AD), when the Muslims defeated the Persians, they captured a huge amount of spoils including the famed jewel-laden royal crown and extremely expensive carpets. The Muslim soldiers brought all the booty to their commander S'ad ibn Abi Waqqas (ra) who in turn sent it fully intact to Caliph 'Umar. When Caliph 'Umar saw the booty, he exclaimed, "Those who did not touch these precious treasures and kept their intention firm are indeed great."

One natural outcome of the belief in the Hereafter is that it gives the believer extraordinary strength and steadfastness to bear the hardship and suffering of this life. The person who does not believe in the Hereafter lacks this strength, resolve and steadfastness. The believer knows that this is not the only life and there is another life which is eternal and has no constrains like those of this life. He believes that this life is very short and transitory and he will be rewarded in the Hereafter for all the difficulties and hardships of this life.

Belief in the Hereafter and longing for Paradise and the sight of Almighty Allah make a person enthused and inspired enough to undergo any hardship. He believes that his body and soul have already been purchased by Allah in lieu of Paradise and its bounties, as Allah has mentioned in the Holy Quran:

إِنَّ ٱللَّهَ ٱشْتَرَىٰ مِنَ ٱلْمُؤْمِنِينَ أَنفُسَهُمْ وَأَمْوَٰلَهُم بِأَنَّ لَهُمُ ٱلْجَنَّةَ يُقَٰتِلُونَ فِى سَبِيلِ ٱللَّهِ فَيَقْتُلُونَ وَيُقْتَلُونَ

Indeed, Allah has purchased from the believers their lives and their properties [in exchange] for what they will have in Paradise; they fight in the cause of Allah, so they kill and are killed. [At-Taubah, 9:111]

This was the spirit which made Muslims restless to sacrifice their lives for the sake of Islam. Here are a few *ahadith* to show the mindset of the Companions of the Prophet (saw) in this respect:

'Abdullah bin Qais reported: While facing the enemy, the Messenger of Allah said: Surely, the gates of Paradise are under the shadow of swords. A man in a shabby condition got up and said to Abu Musa Ash'ari, "Did you hear the Messenger of Allah say this?" Abu Musa Ash'ari said, "Yes!" The narrator said that the person returned to his friends and said, "I greet you (a farewell greeting)." Then he broke the sheath of his sword, threw it away, advanced with his (naked) sword towards the enemy and fought (them) with it until he was martyred. [*Sahih Muslim, Kitab Al-Imara*]

Anas bin Malik reported: Once the Messenger of Allah said, "Get up to enter Paradise which is equal in width to the heavens and the earth." Upon that 'Umair bin al-Humam al-Ansari said, "O Messenger of Allah! Is Paradise equal in extent to the heavens and the earth?" The Messenger of Allah said, "Yes!" 'Umair said, "My goodness!" The Messenger of Allah asked him, "What prompted you to utter these words?" He said, "Messenger of Allah! It is nothing but the desire that I should be among its residents." The Messenger of Allah said, "You are among its residents." 'Umair bin al-Humam then took out dates from his bag and began to eat them. Then he said, "If I were to live until I have eaten all these dates, it would be too long." (The narrator said): He threw away all the dates he had with him. Then he fought the enemies until he was martyred. [*Sahih Muslim, Kitab Al-Imara*]

Anas bin Malik (ra) reported: In the Battle of Uhad, my uncle Anas bin An-Nadr (ra) went to S'ad bin M'uadh (ra) and said, "O S'ad bin M'uadh! By the Lord of An-Nadr, I am smelling fragrance of Paradise coming from the mountain of Uhad." After he (Anas bin An-Nadr) was martyred, he was found to have more than eighty wounds inflicted on his body by swords and arrows. We found him dead and his body was mutilated so badly that none except his sister could recognize him by his fingers. [*Sahih Bukhari, Kitabul Jihad*]

Effects of Disbelief in the Hereafter

The very first outcome of disbelief in the Hereafter is that people become intoxicated with love and greed for worldly possessions. They overindulge in worldly pursuits and spend all of their resources and capabilities in fulfilling their lust and desires. Their appetite for comfort and luxury is never satisfied, as the Holy Quran has mentioned:

$$\text{وَٱلَّذِينَ كَفَرُواْ يَتَمَتَّعُونَ وَيَأْكُلُونَ كَمَا تَأْكُلُ ٱلْأَنْعَـٰمُ وَٱلنَّارُ مَثْوًى لَّهُمْ}$$

Those who disbelieve enjoy themselves and eat as grazing livestock eat, and the Fire will be the residence for them. [Muhammad, 47:12]

أَذْهَبْتُمْ طَيِّبَاتِكُمْ فِى حَيَاتِكُمُ ٱلدُّنْيَا وَٱسْتَمْتَعْتُم بِهَا فَٱلْيَوْمَ تُجْزَوْنَ عَذَابَ ٱلْهُونِ بِمَا كُنتُمْ تَسْتَكْبِرُونَ فِى ٱلْأَرْضِ بِغَيْرِ ٱلْحَقِّ

You exhausted your pleasures during your worldly life and enjoyed them, so this Day you will be awarded the punishment of [extreme] humiliation because you were arrogant upon the earth without right. [Al-Ahqaf, 46:20]

Such people get deceived by the glamor and glitter of the world and their outlook becomes very materialistic and superficial, as the Holy Quran has mentioned:

إِنَّ ٱلَّذِينَ لَا يُؤْمِنُونَ بِٱلْآخِرَةِ زَيَّنَّا لَهُمْ أَعْمَالَهُمْ فَهُمْ يَعْمَهُونَ

Indeed, for those who do not believe in the Hereafter, We have made pleasing to them their deeds, so they wander blindly. [An-Naml, 27:4]

قُلْ هَلْ نُنَبِّئُكُم بِٱلْأَخْسَرِينَ أَعْمَالاً (103) ٱلَّذِينَ ضَلَّ سَعْيُهُمْ فِى ٱلْحَيَوٰةِ ٱلدُّنْيَا وَهُمْ يَحْسَبُونَ أَنَّهُمْ يُحْسِنُونَ صُنْعًا (104) أُوْلَٰئِكَ ٱلَّذِينَ كَفَرُواْ بِـَٔايَٰتِ رَبِّهِمْ وَلِقَآئِهِ فَحَبِطَتْ أَعْمَالُهُمْ فَلَا نُقِيمُ لَهُمْ يَوْمَ ٱلْقِيَٰمَةِ وَزْنًا (105) ذَٰلِكَ جَزَاؤُهُمْ جَهَنَّمُ بِمَا كَفَرُواْ وَٱتَّخَذُوٓاْ ءَايَٰتِى وَرُسُلِى هُزُوًا (06) إِنَّ ٱلَّذِينَ ءَامَنُواْ وَعَمِلُواْ ٱلصَّٰلِحَٰتِ كَانَتْ لَهُمْ جَنَّٰتُ ٱلْفِرْدَوْسِ نُزُلاً (107) خَٰلِدِينَ فِيهَا لَا يَبْغُونَ عَنْهَا حِوَلاً (108)

Say: "Shall we tell you of those who lose most with respect to their deeds?" They are those whose efforts have been wasted in this life, while they thought that they were acquiring good by their works. They are those who deny the signs of their Lord and the fact of their having to meet Him (in the Hereafter). Vain will be their works. Nor shall We, on the Day of Judgment, give them any weight. That is their reward, Hell, because they rejected faith, and took My Signs and My Messengers by way of jest. As to those who believe and work righteous deeds, they have for their entertainment the gardens of Paradise wherein they shall dwell forever and shall not wish to be moved from there. [Al-Kahf, 18:103-108]

People who do not believe in the Hereafter become frivolous about this life and become occupied with sport, entertainment and pastime. Even in the moments of calamity and disaster, they remain occupied in acts of pleasure and amusement, as the Holy Quran has mentioned:

وَذَرِ ٱلَّذِينَ ٱتَّخَذُواْ دِينَهُمْ لَعِبًا وَلَهْوًا وَغَرَّتْهُمُ ٱلْحَيَوٰةُ ٱلدُّنْيَا

Leave alone those who take their religion to be mere play and amusement, and are deceived by the life of this world. [Al-An'am, 6:70]

When they are confronted with calamities and disasters, they only look at the external causes and stop short of finding the real reason. The result is that even the mishaps of catastrophic magnitude fail to wake them up and bring any change in their life, as the Holy Quran mentions in the following verse:

فَلَوْلَآ إِذْ جَاءَهُم بَأْسُنَا تَضَرَّعُواْ وَلَكِن قَسَتْ قُلُوبُهُمْ وَزَيَّنَ لَهُمُ ٱلشَّيْطَانُ مَا كَانُواْ يَعْمَلُونَ

When the suffering reached them from Us, why did not they learn humility? On the contrary, their hearts became hardened and Satan made their (sinful) acts seem alluring to them. [Al-An'am, 6:43]

One of the consequences of disbelief in the Hereafter is that there does not remain any incentive to do any social good unless it entails a worldly benefit or is imposed by circumstances, as the Holy Quran mentions in the following verses:

أَرَءَيْتَ ٱلَّذِى يُكَذِّبُ بِٱلدِّينِ (1) فَذَٰلِكَ ٱلَّذِى يَدُعُّ ٱلْيَتِيمَ (2) وَلَا يَحُضُّ عَلَىٰ طَعَامِ ٱلْمِسْكِينِ (3)

Have you seen the one who denies the Recompense? He drives away the orphan and does not encourage feeding of the poor. [Al-Ma'un, 107:1-3]

If they happen to do something good, it is only to show to others, as the Holy Quran mentions:

وَٱلَّذِينَ يُنفِقُونَ أَمْوَٰلَهُمْ رِئَآءَ ٱلنَّاسِ وَلَا يُؤْمِنُونَ بِٱللَّهِ وَلَا بِٱلْيَوْمِ ٱلْآخِرِ ۗ وَمَن يَكُنِ ٱلشَّيْطَٰنُ لَهُۥ قَرِينًا فَسَآءَ قَرِينًا

And (for) those who spend their wealth only to show to people and do not believe in Allah and the Last Day and whose companion is Satan who is an evil companion. [An-Nisa, 4:38]

كَٱلَّذِى يُنفِقُ مَالَهُۥ رِئَآءَ ٱلنَّاسِ وَلَا يُؤْمِنُ بِٱللَّهِ وَٱلْيَوْمِ ٱلْآخِرِ

Like the one who spends his wealth to show off to people and does not believe in Allah and in the Last Day. [Al-Baqara, 2:264]

It is natural for disbelief in the Hereafter to breed arrogance and haughtiness. If a person does not have the concept of the life after death, what is there to prevent him from acting like an animal without a leash? The worldly laws and regulations may constrain him to some degree, but as soon as those constraints disappear or he finds a way to evade and circumvent them, he starts acting like Pharaoh. That is why the Holy Quran often mentions disbelief in the Hereafter and arrogance together, as in the following verses:

فَٱلَّذِينَ لَا يُؤْمِنُونَ بِٱلْآخِرَةِ قُلُوبُهُم مُّنكِرَةٌ وَهُم مُّسْتَكْبِرُونَ

But those who do not believe in the Hereafter - their hearts are disapproving, and they are arrogant. [An-Nahl, 16:22]

وَٱسْتَكْبَرَ هُوَ وَجُنُودُهُۥ فِى ٱلْأَرْضِ بِغَيْرِ ٱلْحَقِّ وَظَنُّوٓاْ أَنَّهُمْ إِلَيْنَا لَا يُرْجَعُونَ

And he[7] and his hosts were arrogant in the land, without right, and they thought that they would never return to Us. [Al-Qasas, 28:39]

---

[7] Pharaoh

وَقَالَ مُوسَىٰ إِنِّى عُذْتُ بِرَبِّى وَرَبِّكُم مِّن كُلِّ مُتَكَبِّرٍ لَّا يُؤْمِنُ بِيَوْمِ ٱلْحِسَابِ

But Prophet Musa (*alaihis salaam*) said, "Indeed, I have sought refuge in my Lord and your Lord from every arrogant one who does not believe in the Day of Account." [Ghafir, 40:27]

People who do not believe in the Hereafter often face mental agony and spiritual distress. They are often bothered by the thought that this life is going to end one day regardless of how long and how lavishly they live. This feeling keeps them restless and disturbed despite plenty of wealth and luxury and they constantly live in a state of despair and depression.

That is why many of them try to insulate themselves from the thought of death. They do not want anyone to talk about it. They try to forget about it by using drugs and narcotics. They remain in this condition till the very end of their lives. When death finally approaches them, they may wake up, but it becomes too late to change the course of their life. This is what the Holy Quran has mentioned:

قَدْ خَسِرَ ٱلَّذِينَ كَذَّبُواْ بِلِقَاءِ ٱللَّهِ حَتَّىٰ إِذَا جَاءَتْهُمُ ٱلسَّاعَةُ بَغْتَةً قَالُواْ يَٰحَسْرَتَنَا عَلَىٰ مَا فَرَّطْنَا فِيهَا وَهُمْ يَحْمِلُونَ أَوْزَارَهُمْ عَلَىٰ ظُهُورِهِمْ أَلَا سَاءَ مَا يَزِرُونَ

Lost indeed are they who treat it as a falsehood that they must meet Allah, until the hour [of Resurrection] suddenly comes on them; they then say, "Ah! Woe unto us that we took no thought of it"; for they bear their burdens on their backs, and evil indeed are the burdens that they bear. [Al-An'am, 6:31]

وَمَا هَٰذِهِ ٱلْحَيَوٰةُ ٱلدُّنْيَا إِلَّا لَهْوٌ وَلَعِبٌ وَإِنَّ ٱلدَّارَ ٱلْآخِرَةَ لَهِىَ ٱلْحَيَوَانُ لَوْ كَانُواْ يَعْلَمُونَ

This life of the world is but a pastime and amusement; Lo! The home of the Hereafter - that is Life, if they knew. [Al-Ankabut, 29:64]

Epilogue
by
Mohammed Moidul Haque

What has been explained in the preceding pages may be summarized as follows:

1. Allah is the sole creator of every object in the universe including man and *jinn*. Nothing happens in the universe without Allah's permission and knowledge. No one has the ability to do any harm or benefit to anyone without Allah's will and permission. Allah does not need any assistance from anyone in any shape or form to bring anything into existence.

2. Man is Allah's best creation. Allah bestowed man with the highest position among His creations by making him His *khalifah* on the earth.

3. Man is to obey and worship Allah whereas all other creations are appointed to serve man.

4. Man has been placed on the earth to test whether he obeys Allah or follows his vain desires. Other creations such as the sun, moon, earth, sky, mountains, trees, oceans, etc. have not been given freedom to obey or disobey Allah; they are in full submission to Allah. But man has been given freedom to do what he wants – obey Allah or follow his desires.

5. This life is very short and transitory whereas the Life Hereafter is everlasting with limitless bounties and miseries.

6. This world will be dismantled one day; everyone will be resurrected and accounted for all of his deeds; and everyone will be rewarded and punished accordingly.

7. The Life Hereafter is an abode of comfort and luxury for those who obey Allah in this life and a place of misery and torture for those who disobey Him.

8. Allah sent prophets to make man aware of Himself, the Life Hereafter, His orders, what He expects of man and the consequences of man's actions.

124

9. Prophet Adam (*alahis salaam*) was the first prophet and Prophet Muhammad (saw) was the last prophet. The chain of prophethood ended with Prophet Muhammad (saw).

10. The Holy Quran is the final Book of revelation. Thus the Holy Quran and Prophet Muhammad (saw) are the final source of guidance for mankind until the Last Day.

Since Prophet Muhammad (saw) was the final prophet, the responsibility of guiding mankind to Allah and His divine religion rests on the shoulders of the followers of Prophet Muhammad (saw), as the Holy Quran mentions:

كُنتُمْ خَيْرَ أُمَّةٍ أُخْرِجَتْ لِلنَّاسِ تَأْمُرُونَ بِالْمَعْرُوفِ وَتَنْهَوْنَ عَنِ الْمُنكَرِ وَتُؤْمِنُونَ بِاللَّهِ

You are the best nation ever raised for mankind; you enjoin good, forbid wrong and believe in Allah [Al-Imran, 3:110]

Thus Muslims have two responsibilities: 1) to practice Islam in their own lives and 2) invite others to the same. The Companions of Prophet Muhammad (saw) fulfilled these responsibilities in the most exemplary way as a result of which they gained an unprecedented degree of success in both this life and the Life Hereafter. Their mission was not to conquer land, accumulate wealth or gain dominance. Their mission was to please Allah, benefit humanity and guide people to the real success which has been defined by the Holy Quran in the following verse:

كُلُّ نَفْسٍ ذَآئِقَةُ الْمَوْتِ وَإِنَّمَا تُوَفَّوْنَ أُجُورَكُمْ يَوْمَ الْقِيَامَةِ فَمَن زُحْزِحَ عَنِ النَّارِ وَأُدْخِلَ الْجَنَّةَ فَقَدْ فَازَ وَمَا الْحَيَوٰةُ الدُّنْيَآ إِلَّا مَتَاعُ الْغُرُورِ

Every soul has to taste death; and only on the Day of Judgment shall you be paid your full recompense. Only he who is saved from the Fire and admitted to the Garden will have attained the object (of Life); the life of this world is but goods and chattels of deception. [Al-Imran, 3:185]

It is unfortunate that Muslims today have forgotten the purpose of their life, the responsibility that lies on their shoulders due to being the *ummah* of Prophet Muhammad (saw) and the true secret of success. They have become like a person who is sitting on a precious treasure and is neither benefiting himself nor letting others benefit from it.

May Allah give us true understanding of Islam, *Tawheed, aakhirah,* and *khat-mun-nabuwah*[1] (finality of prophethood)! I hope and pray that this book provides a solid foundation for the same.

---

[1] ختم النبوة

Glossary of Arabic Terms

aakhirah – آخرة - Life Hereafter

ahadith – احاديث - sayings and practices of Prophet Muhammad; it is the plural of hadith

'alim – عالم - Islamic scholar

'aqeedah – عقيدة - belief system, faith

arkaan – اركان - basic rituals, plural of rukn which means ritual

as-Samad - الصمد - self-sufficing

Baitullah – بيت الله - House of Allah, the cube-shaped structure in Makkah

barakah - بركة - blessing

barzakh - برزخ - the state in which a person will remain after his death until the Day of Resurrection

bid'ah - بدعة - illegitimate innovation

darood - درود - salutation on prophets

d'awah - دعوة - calling people towards Allah and His religion

deen – دين - religion, Islam, way of life, creed, judgment

d'ua – دعا - supplication, prayer

dunya – دنيا - worldly life; worldly pursuit

fitrah – فطرة - nature, disposition

ghaib - غيب - unseen

hadith – حديث – saying or practice of Prophet Muhammad (saw)

haq - حق – truth

halaal - حلال - permissble

haraam - حرام - forbidden

Haram – حرم - area surrounding Baitullah

hijrah - هجرة - emigration

'ibadah - عبادة - worship, prayer

ihsan - احسان - full consciousness of Allah's presence

ikhlas - اخلاص - sincerity

iman – ايمان - belief, faith

islah - اصلاح - reform

istighfar - استغفار - repentance for wrongdoings

K'aba – كعبه - house of Allah

khair - خير - goodness, benefit

khalifah – خليفة - vicegerent, deputy

kufr – كفر - atheism, disbelief, rejection of faith

madaaris – مدارس - plural of madrasah

madrasah – مدرسة - school of Islamic learning

masaajid - مساجد - places of worship; it is plural of

masjid - مسجد - place of worship

momin – مومن - believer

momineen – مومنين - plural of momin, belivers

mushrik – مشرك - polytheist

mushrikin - مشركين - is the plural of mushrik

niyah - نية - intention

qadr – قدر - destiny

qisas - قصاص - compensation

rak'ah - ركعة - unit of salah

risalah - رسالة - prophethood

salah - صلوة - prayer

salawaat - صلوات - prayer, benediction, blessing

seerah – سيرة - way of life

shari'ah - شريعة - Islamic code of conduct

shirk - شرك - polytheism

silm - سلم - peace, submission

suluk - سلوك - traditions of spiritual training and mentoring

sunnah – سنة - saying and practice of the Prophet (saw)

tabligh – تبليغ - propagation of Allah's religion

taghut -- طاغوت - every object (besides Allah) that may be considered
        worthy of worshipping or submission

taqwa -- تقوى – piety

tariqat - طريقت - traditions of spiritual training and mentoring

tasawwuf – تصوف – mysticism

tashahhud - تشهد - sitting position in prayers

tawaaf – طواف - circumambulation around K'aba

Tawheed - توحيد - oneness of Allah

'ulama – علماء - it is the plural of 'alim; scholars of Islam

ummah - امة - nation

wahi - وحى - divine revelation

wudhu - وضو - washing of hands, face and feet before prayer

yaqeen - يقين - conviction

zakah – زكوة - obligatory poor-due

zuhd - زهد - asceticism from worldly pleasures

Index of Quranic Verses

Index of People, Places, Etc.

Made in the USA
Monee, IL
07 July 2026

56551368R00085